The American Revolution

Reader

Core Knowledge®

ISBN: 978-1-68380-022-4

The American Revolution

Table of Contents

The American Revolution

Reader

Core Knowledge History and Geography™

Chapter 1
Meet the Colonists

The Big Question

In what ways did the colonies change over time?

Coming to Pennsylvania On a pleasant summer day in 1750, a ship carrying four hundred Germans arrived at the docks in Philadelphia. These newcomers were about to begin their new lives in a new place.

Vocabulary

immigrant, n. a person from one country who moves to another country to live

colony, n. an area, region, or country that is controlled and settled by people from another country

Even a hundred years earlier, the arrival of four hundred **immigrants** was not big news. Back then, many people wanted to start a new life in an English **colony**. At the time there were five English colonies in North America.

By 1750, there were thirteen English colonies on the East Coast of what became the United States. All of them were strong and growing. Almost every week, a ship arrived with more immigrants. The population of the colonies had already passed one million and was quickly climbing toward two million. Settlements had spread from the Atlantic Ocean to as far west as the Appalachian Mountains.

Immigrants by the hundreds arrived in the American colonies in the 1700s.

Why had so many people come to the British colonies in North America? Why were so many still coming in 1750? The answer is simply opportunity: the opportunity to own land of their own, the opportunity to work in the growing towns and cities, the opportunity to worship as they pleased, the opportunity to escape the past and start a new life.

Who were these colonists? Where were they from? They were mainly ordinary people—farmers and people from small towns. Most colonists were from England, but a large number—almost a third—came from Germany. Many others came from Scotland, Ireland, Wales, Sweden, and the Netherlands.

Not all of those who **migrated** to the colonies traveled willingly. About one person in five was enslaved, having been forcefully removed from his or her home in Africa. Most eventually found themselves in the South, but there were enslaved people in the North, too. Almost none of the people who came from Africa were free.

Vocabulary

migrate, v. to move from one place to another to live

Life in the Colonies

More than nine out of ten colonial families lived on farms. They farmed their land by themselves. Every member of the family had a job to do. As a result, they produced nearly everything they needed to survive. They raised their own food. They made their own clothes and their own tools. They made their own furniture. Most of them even built the houses that they lived in. When the weather and the harvest were good, farmers sometimes had enough food left over to sell.

Colonists made almost everything they needed for themselves.

In the mid-1700s, there were still only four or five cities in all of the colonies, and just a handful of towns. These cities were small by today's standards, but they were growing quickly. In just a few short years, Philadelphia would become the second-largest city in the whole British Empire next to London, England.

What sparked this growth of towns and cities? **Trade** within the colonies and with other countries was the driving factor. From the docks of the cities on the East Coast, **merchants** sent lumber, fur, salted fish, flour, rice, indigo, and tobacco to many parts of the world. To those docks, ships returned with glass, paint, tea, wine, and other goods the colonists needed or wanted.

Vocabulary

trade, n. the exchange or sale of goods or services.

merchant, n. a person who sells or trades goods

Trade also meant jobs. Men loaded and unloaded ships. They built boats. They made sails, rope, and barrels for shipping goods. The cities and towns offered other kinds of work, too. Men, and some women, ran stores and shops. Skilled workers baked bread and made pots and pans. Others printed newspapers or made fine shoes and clothes for other city dwellers.

Staying Apart and Coming Together

When immigrants arrived in the colonies, they preferred to settle near people who were from the same country. This made them feel more comfortable in a strange, new land. They could speak their own language and follow their own traditional ways of life. They wore the same kinds of clothing they had worn in their homeland and built the same kinds of houses.

In time, however, something interesting and important happened. Immigrant groups began to borrow ideas and **customs** from each other. For example, consider the log cabin. Swedes had built log cabins in their homeland. In the colonies, they found plenty of trees that could be used to build homes. A log cabin was easy to build. Two strong settlers with axes could build one in a couple of weeks. Other groups came to North America with their own ideas of how to build a house. When they saw the log cabins built by Swedish settlers, they realized that these homes were perfect for life on the **frontier**. Soon settlers from many different countries built log cabins like the ones built by the Swedes.

Vocabulary

custom, n. a traditional way of acting or doing something

frontier, n. where newly settled areas adjoin unsettled areas or the wilderness

A log cabin could make a snug home for a frontier family.

This borrowing of ideas and customs among immigrant groups even changed the way colonists spoke. Most colonists spoke English, but English speakers began to borrow words from the other languages spoken in the colonies. They borrowed the words *noodle* and *pretzel* from German. They borrowed the words *waffle, cookie,* and *sleigh* from Dutch. The words *pecan, moccasin, skunk,* and *squash* came from Native American languages. Words such as *yams, banjo,* and *tote* came from African languages.

The use of words borrowed from other languages created a new form of English that would eventually be called *American English*. Little by little, this new American English became the language of the children and grandchildren of immigrants from other lands.

Better Roads

By the 1750s, the colonists were also being brought together by improved roads. These roads were not very good compared to our own. They were narrow, often muddy, and filled with tree stumps. Still, they were better than the roads of fifty or a hundred years earlier. These roads made it easier to travel through the colonies. Easier travel led to increased trade among the colonies.

Better roads also improved communications by speeding up the exchange of information. In the mid-1750s, mail delivery between Philadelphia and Boston increased to once a week instead of every two weeks. That meant that newspapers printed in the cities could be delivered to colonists in the countryside more easily. Colonists could now read the same news and stay informed about the same things.

In all these ways, colonists of many different backgrounds were starting to come together. They were beginning—just beginning, of course—to have more things in common. This coming together soon became *very* important.

The Thirteen English Colonies of North America

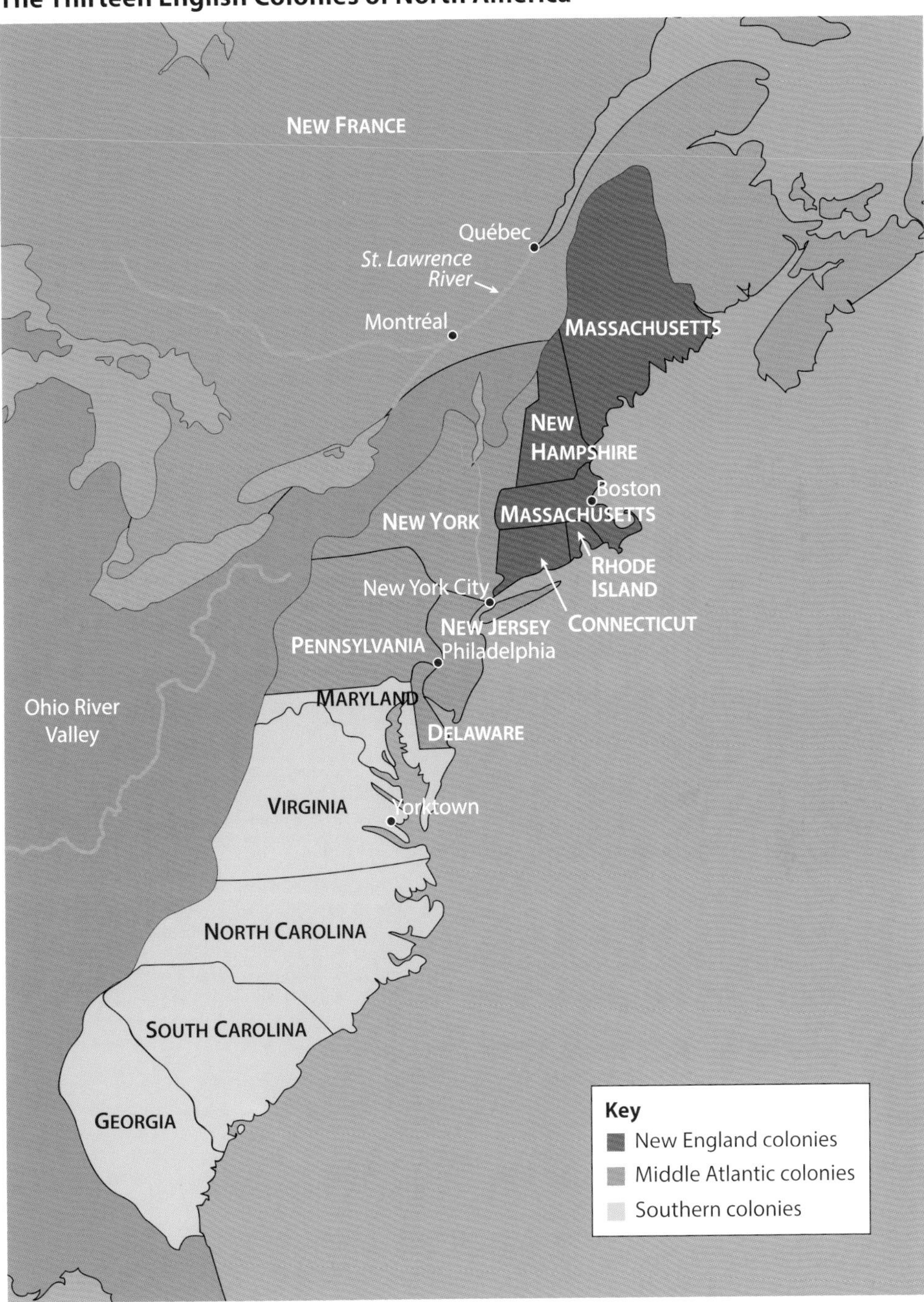

By the mid-1700s, English colonies covered much of eastern North America.

Chapter 2
If You Had Lived in the Colonies

Growing Up What would it have been like to grow up in the colonies? Let's spend a little time finding out. We'll begin by imagining that you are a colonist, and what your family and daily life look like. Your family probably lives on a farm. Nine out of ten colonial families live on farms.

> **The Big Question**
>
> What was daily life like for free colonial children growing up on a farm, in comparison to enslaved children?

Chances are, your house is pretty crowded. That's because colonists have large families. You have lots of brothers and sisters.

What are the chances that you have your own bedroom? Just about zero. You not only don't have your own bedroom; you don't even have your own bed. You share a bed or a straw mattress on the floor with other children in the family.

Many colonial children had lots of brothers and sisters.

While the house is crowded, you are grateful to have so many kids in the family. You don't have neighborhood friends, because you don't have a neighborhood. Only people living in villages and towns have neighbors, so your brothers and sisters are your "built-in" playmates.

Of course everyone has regular chores to do. That includes you. Everyone's day begins at dawn, if not before.

If you are a boy, your first job is to bring in firewood and build the fire. Matches don't exist yet, so you hope there is still a burning coal in the fireplace from the night before. If not, you have to start a new fire.

After breakfast and morning prayers, you head out to the fields with your father. You plant and hoe and clear away brush from new land that's to be planted next year. You even help repair a fence or two.

Colonial children worked hard.

If you are a girl, you help your mother make candles and preserve foods, starting right after breakfast. Your chores probably also include feeding the animals. The rest of your morning is spent helping cook the noon meal. In the afternoon, you sew, knit, weave, or spin yarn.

Did you notice there is no time in your day's schedule for school? That's because you probably don't go to school. Perhaps you did last year and the year before, but you can read and write now. Most colonial parents feel that once you can do that, you don't need any more school.

Chances are though, you learn to read and write at home. An older brother or sister or maybe a parent teaches you when you are five or six. If no one in your family can read, then you might be sent to learn at another farmhouse where someone else can. It is considered important to learn how to read.

Children of Enslaved People

If you are a child in an **enslaved** family on a **plantation**, your life is different. When you are quite young—say five or six—there is plenty of time for play. In fact, some of your playmates are probably the children of the plantation owner. You may fish, pick berries, and freely explore the plantation fields together.

Vocabulary

enslaved, adj. forced to become a slave

plantation, n. a large farm where cash crops are grown by the person who owns the land

Then, when you reach seven or eight years old, you start to take care of younger brothers and sisters. Also, the plantation owner begins to give you jobs like sweeping the yard, feeding the chickens, and collecting the eggs. Even at this age, however, you start to understand that you do not have the same freedoms as the plantation owner's children.

Enslaved people working in the fields.

The big change in your life comes when you are about ten years old. Now you begin life as an enslaved worker. You work in the fields doing the same hard work as the adults. You plant, plow, and pick cotton from sunup to sundown.

Unlike the plantation owner's children, you probably can't read. Depending on the colony you live in, the law may actually forbid anyone from teaching you to read.

Sickness and Cures

Sickness is a serious problem in every colonial home. Many children die from **disease**. Little is really known about why people get sick or how they can get well and stay well.

> **Vocabulary**
>
> **disease,** n. sickness
>
> **herb,** n. a plant used to give food flavor or as medicine

A lot of people think they know, though. They make their own medicines from plants called **herbs** and also from the roots and bark of trees. Do you have a cut that isn't healing? Swelling that won't go down? A bad cold, perhaps? There's sure to be an herb or a root that will cure you.

Some of these herbs have been used for hundreds of years and really do seem to help. Others, though, are not so helpful.

There are also some special tricks that are supposed to help you get better. For example, to bring down a fever, your parents might cut your toenails, put the clippings in a small linen bag, and tie the bag around the neck of an eel, before putting the eel in a tub of water. When the eel dies, your fever supposedly goes down. One of the best-educated men in the Massachusetts colony recommends that cure.

Even if you are just feeling tired, there's a special recipe to help. You roast a toad and grind it up. Then you add boiling water to make a kind of tea. Drink it and you'll be feeling lively in no time. For a cold or sore throat, sprinkle pepper on a piece of meat and wrap it around your throat.

COLONIAL CURES

1. *Feed your children only plain foods and not so much sugar, spice, or salt. No eating between meals, except for dry bread.*
2. *Keep them away from candy.*
3. *See that they sleep on a hard bed. No soft feathers.*
4. *Bathe them in cold water, even in the winter.*
5. *Give them very thin shoes that will leak and let in water. (A famous man got this idea by noting that poor people often went barefoot and didn't seem to get sick from that.)*
6. *Strawberries, cherries, and gooseberries are good for children. Melons, peaches, plums, and grapes are not, even though they are tasty. Don't give them any.*

Of course, you could go to a doctor. There are a few doctors in the colonies, but visiting one probably won't do much good. There are no special schools for training doctors in the colonies. Doctors don't know much more than most others about making people well. Doctors do have a favorite cure for almost any illness, though. It's called *bleeding the patient*. To do this, doctors cut a vein in the patient's arm to let blood come out. Of course, the best thing to do is to stay well.

Chapter 3
The Rights of Englishmen

Part of the Empire If the colonists had bumper stickers, one of them surely would have said, "Proud to be British." That's how most colonists felt in the middle of the 1700s.

The Big Question

What were some of the rights granted to the citizens of the British Empire?

They were members of what became the greatest empire in the world—the British Empire. They even modeled their own governing bodies on the British system. How did a small island nation create the British Empire? Beginning in the 1500s, what was then the English Crown gave permission for people to set up colonies in North America. Over time, England's colonies in North America grew. In 1707, England, Wales, and Scotland united under the name of Great Britain. Great Britain later set up other colonies in places like Africa and India. Within a few hundred years, Great Britain became a powerful nation with colonies all over the world. In other words, it created an **empire**.

Vocabulary

empire, n. a group of countries or territories ruled by an all-powerful authority such as a monarch

The colonists were inspired by the parliamentary system. The English Parliament has two houses, the House of Lords and the House of Commons. This is a House of Commons meeting during the eighteenth century.

As members of the British Empire, the colonists had special trade agreements with other parts of the empire. On the oceans, their ships were protected by the British navy, the greatest navy in the world. Most important, the colonists in North America enjoyed a great deal of **self-government**. That is, the colonists had a say in choosing their own laws. How did that happen?

> **Vocabulary**
>
> **self-government,** n. the ability of people to rule themselves and make their own laws
>
> **English Parliament,** n. the original law-making branch of the English government that is made up of the House of Lords and the House of Commons

Self-government started in England several hundred years earlier. At that time, certain wealthy and important English landowners elected people to represent them in the **English Parliament**. Parliament is a law-making body, much like our **Congress**.

At first, Parliament had little power. The king had most of it. Over time, members of Parliament insisted that only they, not the king, should make decisions about **taxes** and spending. They said that Parliament should have a say in other decisions, too.

English kings disagreed. For a few hundred years, the kings and Parliament struggled over this issue. In 1689, Parliament finally won.

> **Vocabulary**
>
> **Congress,** n. the law-making branch of the American government that is made up of the House of Representatives and the Senate
>
> **tax,** n. money that people are required to pay to support the workings of the government

When the English first settled in North America, they brought with them the idea of self-government. Pretty soon, colonists were electing **representatives** to their own law-making bodies. These bodies were usually called **assemblies**. But not everyone in the colonies could vote. Women, African Americans, and Native Americans could not vote. Only white men who owned enough property could vote. This meant that a large part of the colonial population could not vote.

> **Vocabulary**
>
> **representative,** n. a person who is chosen or elected to speak on the behalf of other people
>
> **assembly,** n. a group of representatives who gather to make laws

Soon colonists insisted that only their elected assemblies could make laws for their colonies. They knew it was Parliament's job

Colonists wanted their own elected assemblies.

to run the whole British Empire. It was up to Parliament to pass laws about trade among different parts of the empire. Only Parliament could decide the rules for trade between the empire and other parts of the world. The American colonists didn't argue with that.

When it came to everyday life in their own colonies, however, the colonists began to think that only they knew what was best for them.

Claiming British Rights

As you have discovered, England had joined with Scotland and Wales to form the nation of Great Britain. The people of Great Britain—the English, the Scots, and the Welsh—had self-government. They also had other rights and liberties. As members of the British Empire, colonists in North America felt they should have the same rights.

Most of these rights and liberties were meant to protect the people against unfair actions by their own government. For example, the government could not just take away a person's house or land or ship or other property. If the government said it needed that property for a very important purpose, it had to prove that to a judge. If the judge agreed with the government, the government had to pay the owner for whatever it was taking.

Similarly, government officers could not search your home or business whenever they felt like it. They first had to explain to a judge why they believed you were hiding something illegal. The judge then had to give permission for the officers to conduct a search. Otherwise no search was allowed.

According to the law, British citizens could not be put in jail unless they were accused of breaking a law. If they were accused, they could not be kept in jail indefinitely. They had the right to a trial before a jury of fellow **citizens**.

Vocabulary

citizen, n. a person who is legally recognized as a member or subject of a country or state

There were other rights, too. If citizens wanted to gather peacefully to talk about a problem or to protest something, the government could not stop them. If they wanted to petition their government, they had that right, too. To petition the government is to ask the government to change a law, or to do something, or even to stop doing something.

Do these rights seem very special to you? Maybe not. We have them in the United States today, and sometimes we take them for granted. Even today, many people in the world do not enjoy these rights. In the middle of the 1700s, very few people outside of the British Empire did. The people of Great Britain were proud to have "the rights of Englishmen." So were the colonists.

No wonder the colonists felt they were among the most fortunate people on earth. They lived in a land blessed by nature. They enjoyed rights and liberties equal to anyone, anywhere in the world. They were proud and happy to be a part of the empire of Great Britain. The idea of separating from the British Empire probably never entered the minds of most colonists. Many years later, Benjamin Franklin said, “I never heard in any conversation from any person . . . the least [desire] for separation from England.”

Franklin was remembering how the colonists felt around 1763. But thirteen years later the American colonies separated from Britain and declared their **independence**. What happened to make the colonists change their minds?

Vocabulary

independence, n. freedom from the control of a person or group of people

Life was better than it had been in Europe for many colonists.

Chapter 4
Learning Hard Lessons

Whose Land Is It? Traveling hundreds of miles through the wilderness was a long way to go to deliver a message. It must have seemed especially long to the twenty-one-year-old military officer from Virginia who delivered the message. All he got for his troubles was a big "No."

The Big Question

What were some of the mistakes young George Washington made when dealing with the French army?

Vocabulary

militia, n. a group of armed citizens prepared for military service at any time

fort, n. a protected building or place that is generally used by the military as a stronghold

governor, n. a person appointed by the king to oversee a region or colony

The young officer and his party of six were from the British colony of Virginia. They were members of the Virginia **militia**, a sort of volunteer citizen's army. The year was 1753. France had just built a string of **forts** along the Ohio River in what is now western Pennsylvania. The young officer's mission was to carry a message from the **governor** of Virginia to the French general in charge of those forts.

The French and the British built forts in North America.

For weeks the Virginians traveled by horseback and canoe until they finally met up with the French general. The young officer handed him the message. The main idea of the message was simple: Your forts are on Virginia's land. Get out!

The French general was polite but firm. "No," he replied. "My troops will not get out. This land belongs to France. French fur trappers have lived on this land for a hundred years. French colonists have settled here. We will not leave."

On the return journey to Virginia, the group's horses gave out, forcing the officer and his men to walk. Along the way, a Native American fired at the officer. The shot barely missed him. Then while crossing an ice-filled river on a raft, the officer was accidentally knocked overboard. He nearly drowned before his men got him out.

The men finally returned to Virginia, and the officer gave the governor the bad news. The French were determined to stay.

The young officer's unsuccessful journey would soon lead to war. The war led to events that brought about the birth of the United States of America.

Who was the twenty-one-year-old officer from the Virginia colony? His name was George Washington. He would have a lot to do with the birth of the United States of America.

Washington's Mistakes

The governor of the Virginia colony was determined to make the French leave the land near the Ohio River. If they could achieve this, Virginia would have more control of the Ohio River and the smaller rivers that flowed from and fed into the larger river. One year later, in 1754, he sent George Washington to the west again. This time Washington led a force of 150 men.

George Washington was proud to be an officer in the Virginia militia.

The British had built a small fort in western Pennsylvania on the site of present-day Pittsburgh. The fort sat where two rivers come together to form the Ohio River. Washington was to join forces with the British soldiers at the fort. Before he arrived, Washington learned that the French had already captured the British fort and renamed it Fort Duquesne (/doo*kayn/).

In time, George Washington would become a great **general**, but in 1754, he was young and inexperienced. He made a number of mistakes. Washington did not have enough men to drive the French out of the fort. The wisest thing to do would have been to return to Virginia. Instead, he continued on with his small force.

Vocabulary

general, n. the main leader of an army

Along the way, Washington's troops surprised and defeated a group of thirty French soldiers, killing ten of them. The French at Fort Duquesne had many more men than Washington had, and they had Shawnee and Delaware Native American **allies** as well. They were sure to send out a larger force from the fort to deal with Washington's Virginians.

> **Vocabulary**
>
> **ally,** n. a nation that promises to help another nation in wartime

Realizing this, Washington built a makeshift camp southeast of the French stronghold. His men called the camp "Fort Necessity." The spot Washington chose for Fort Necessity was a low piece of ground. Soon after the French attacked, it began to rain heavily. Before long, Washington's men, their guns, and their gunpowder were soaked with the rain that collected in the low area where the fort was built. The Virginians fought bravely, but after nine hours, Washington was forced to surrender.

The French commander instructed an assistant to prepare a statement explaining why the fighting had taken place. The statement said, "We, the Virginians, are the ones who started the fighting. It was all our fault." The French commander read the statement and handed it to Washington. "Sign," he said. "Sign, or I will not allow the prisoners to return to Virginia." Washington signed, and the men were released.

When the men returned to Virginia, British officials were very angry. They were angry with the French and angry with

Washington. They blamed him for his unwise decisions. They also blamed him for signing the statement. Washington resigned from the Virginia militia. That could have been the end of his military career. If it had been, you might be saluting the British flag today instead of the Stars and Stripes.

Chapter 5
The French and Indian War

A War in the Colonies Washington's small battle against the French started the French and Indian War. On one side was France, their French colonists in North America, and their Native American allies. On the other side was Great Britain, their British colonists in North America, and their Native American allies.

> **The Big Question**
>
> How did the British defeat the French in the French and Indian War?

Great Britain and France had been fighting each other on and off for nearly a hundred years. No one was surprised that they were at war again. The two European countries had colonies all over the world. Both wanted to control the other's colonies. It was no surprise when the war that began in North America spread to two other continents and the Atlantic, Pacific, and Indian Oceans. In Europe and Asia, the war was called the Seven Years' War. In North America, it was called the French and Indian War.

GREAT BRITAIN

FRANCE

George Washington's small battle helped trigger another war between Great Britain and France.

Fighting in the Woods

> **Vocabulary**
>
> **colonel,** n. a high-ranking military official
>
> **parade,** n. a public display of people moving in a long line
>
> **advance,** v. to move forward

The British were determined to take Fort Duquesne and drive the French out of the Ohio River Valley. In 1755, they sent General Edward Braddock with 2,200 soldiers from the British army to do the job. Eager to join Braddock's army and return to Fort Duquesne, George Washington offered his services to the British general. Braddock appointed the eager young Virginian to the position of **colonel** (/ker*null/). Washington was put in charge of 450 colonial soldiers.

Braddock was an experienced general. He knew how to fight wars in Europe, where armies battled on great open fields. He knew very little about fighting a war in the woods of North America. Even worse, he was too stubborn to listen to anyone who did.

The first thing Braddock did was order his men to cut a hundred-mile-long road through the woods toward Fort Duquesne. His army would march on the road—almost as if they were on **parade**.

Colonel Washington knew that building the road was unwise. He and his colonists knew about the woods. They warned Braddock that his soldiers should **advance** with great caution. An attack could come at any moment from anywhere. Braddock ignored their advice. They were only colonists. What did they know about the art of war?

A few miles from Fort Duquesne, French soldiers and their Native American allies attacked Braddock's army without warning. They fired from hiding places in the thick woods. The British didn't

Both sides had Native American allies. The Huron fought with the French; the Iroquois sided with the British.

know what hit them. Their bright red coats made them easy targets. They panicked and ran. General Braddock was killed.

Fortunately for the British, George Washington had joined them. Courageously exposing himself to danger, Washington led the remaining British soldiers to safety.

Victory for the British

For a time, the French and Indian War went badly for the British elsewhere too. Things began to turn around when William Pitt became the British **prime minister**. As prime minister, Pitt was in charge of Great Britain's foreign affairs. This included foreign wars and dealing with the colonies.

> **Vocabulary**
>
> **prime minister,** n. the head of the government in some countries

It was true that the war was being fought around the world, not just in North America. But Pitt knew the American colonies were valuable to Great Britain. He decided that Great Britain must win the war and keep control of its North American lands. If that meant sending more soldiers to North America, Pitt would do it. Waging a war on many continents was expensive, but Pitt was ready to spend whatever was necessary to win.

Pitt wanted to win control of two rivers: the St. Lawrence River and the Niagara River. The French used these rivers to send supplies to their soldiers near the Great Lakes and in the Ohio River Valley, including those at Fort Duquesne. If the British could prevent the French from using these rivers, they would soon run out of supplies.

Aided by their Native American allies and the American colonists, the British did what Pitt wanted. In addition, British and American forces captured Fort Duquesne. They renamed it Fort Pitt. That is how the city of Pittsburgh eventually got its name. They also captured the French fortress at Louisbourg in Canada.

Another part of Pitt's plan was to capture Quebec. The city of Quebec sits atop steep cliffs alongside the St. Lawrence River. The cliffs protected the city from attack. At least, that's what the French thought. One night in September 1759, British soldiers, led by General James Wolfe, climbed to the top of the cliffs. When dawn broke, the French found the British assembled on a flat area, called the Plains of Abraham, ready for battle. The British defeated the French forces and took the city of Quebec. Both Wolfe and the French general, Louis Montcalm, died in the battle.

The British now controlled the St. Lawrence River, and the French had lost. The French and Indian War ended when Great Britain and France signed the Treaty of Paris in 1763. As a part of the **peace treaty**, France gave all

Vocabulary

"peace treaty," (phrase), an agreement between two or more groups to bring an end to fighting, conflict, or war between themselves

of Canada to Great Britain. France also gave the land it had claimed between the Appalachian Mountains and the Mississippi River to Britain. The land west of the Mississippi River was given to Spain, one of France's allies in the war. Spain was, however, forced to give up Florida.

How complete was Great Britain's victory? Britain was now the main colonial power in North America.

Colonial North America After the French and Indian War

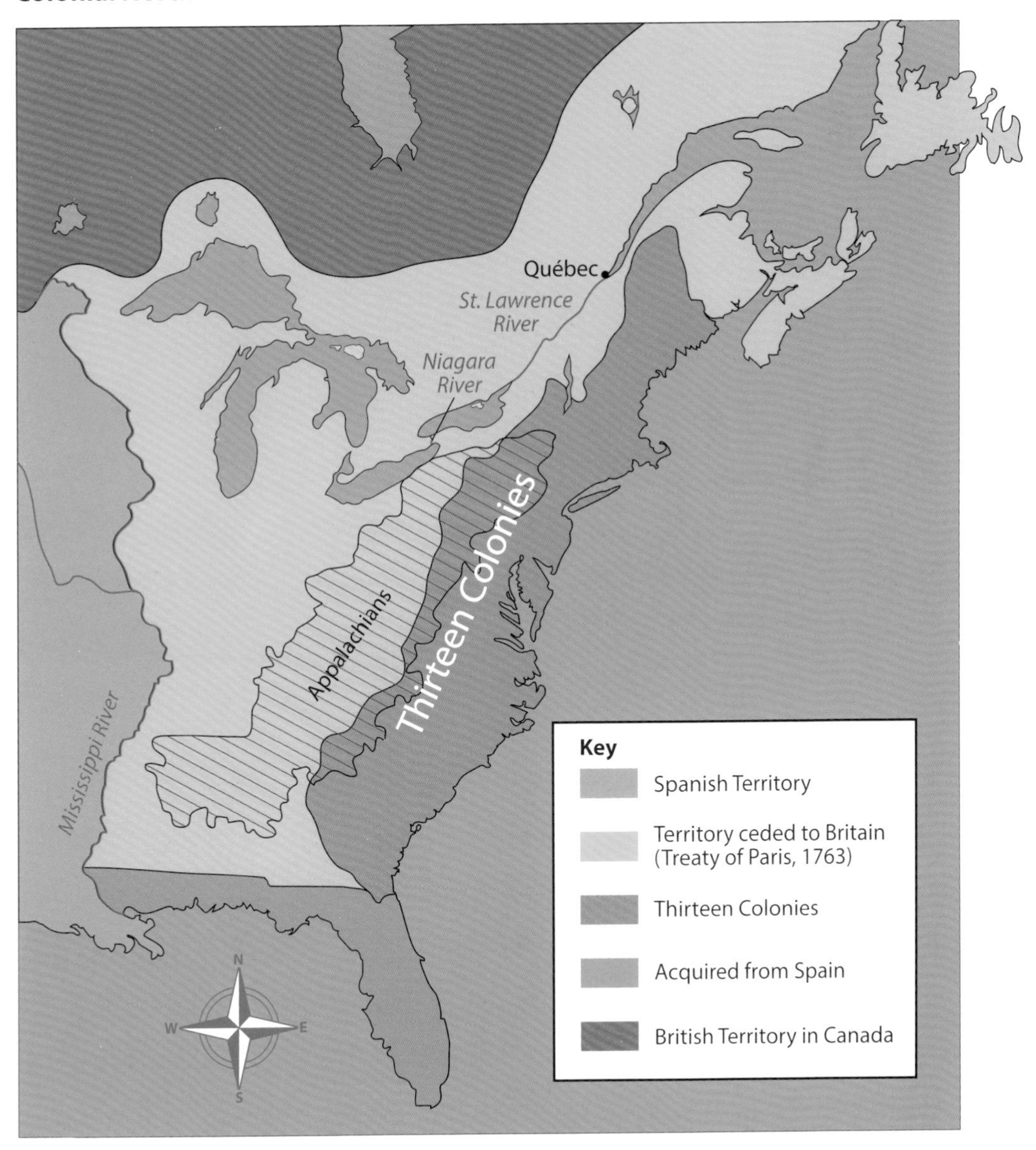

This map shows the lands gained at the end of the French and Indian War. Spain had joined the war on the side of France. It had to give up land, too.

Chapter 6
The Quarrel with Britain Begins

Colonists Claim New Land What's the point of winning land in a war if you're not allowed to use it? Even before the French and Indian War, some colonists had moved onto the lands west of the Appalachian Mountains.

The Big Question

What were the reasons why George III would not allow the colonists to move west into the Ohio River Valley?

The colonists wanted to move onto land in the Ohio River Valley and set up farms.

Now that France had given up its claim to land in the Ohio River Valley and beyond, many colonists looked forward to using the land themselves. The British government saw the matter differently. Many groups of Native Americans lived on that land. Some of them had fought with the British in the war against France. Having just ended one war with France, the British did not want to start a new one with Native Americans. They would surely have one, though, if colonists kept pushing onto Native American lands. In fact, one conflict did break out among Native Americans, settlers, and British soldiers. This conflict was called *Pontiac's War.* During this rebellion, Native Americans in the Great Lakes area tried to drive settlers off of their land.

Great Britain believed that it would be best to keep colonists away from Native American lands—for now, at least. On a map of North America, the British king, George III, drew a line running along the Appalachian Mountains from New York all the way south to Georgia. He then issued a **proclamation**. Until further notice, no more colonists were allowed to settle west of that line.

Vocabulary

proclamation, n. an important official announcement that is usually made to the public

The Proclamation of 1763 angered the colonists. They had not fought the French to win land for Native Americans. They expected to keep it for themselves. Now their own king was telling them they couldn't settle there. The king also said that thousands of British soldiers would stay along the frontier to enforce the proclamation. The presence of British soldiers meant colonists couldn't move west of George III's line.

Native Americans did not want the colonists to move onto their land.

The Quarrel Grows

Soon the colonists had an even bigger disagreement with Great Britain. This new quarrel also grew from the war with France.

Britain spent a lot of money to win the French and Indian War. In fact, it spent more money than the British government really had. The government had borrowed what it needed to pay for the war. Now it had to pay back the borrowed money. It also needed to pay for the soldiers on the North American frontier.

Where was this money going to come from? Parliament thought the colonists should pay—maybe not all of the money, but certainly a fair share. The colonists had been helped by Britain's victory over France. They should help pay for it.

First, Parliament said colonists needed to start paying the taxes they *should* have been paying all along. For example, colonists were supposed to pay taxes on certain **imported** goods. Instead, they had been smuggling—bringing in the goods secretly—to avoid the **tax collectors**.

The British government sent more officials to the colonies to make sure the colonists paid their taxes. The officials were especially interested in new taxes on sugar and **molasses**. These officials could enter and search colonists' homes and businesses without the owners' permission. They could search for smuggled goods or anything else that showed colonists had broken the law.

Vocabulary

import, v. to bring in goods to one country from another country

tax collector, n. a person appointed by the government who is responsible for collecting taxes from citizens

molasses, n. thick, dark, sticky syrup made from sugar

Remember the "rights of Englishmen"? One of those rights said that government officials could not just search a home or business whenever they felt like it. How could the British government take this right away from its colonists?

Parliament found another way to make colonists pay. When the French and Indian War ended, there were thousands of British soldiers in the colonies. The British government wanted to keep them there. To help pay for this, Parliament passed the Quartering Act. The act required colonial governments to supply quarters for the British soldiers. Quarters were places to live.

The colonists did not like the Quartering Act. Why did the British government want to keep soldiers in the colonies? If it was for the colonists' protection, whom were they being protected from? Were the soldiers staying in the colonies to make sure that colonists obeyed British laws, even the unfair ones?

Many colonists did not like having to quarter British soldiers in their homes.

Chapter 7
The Stamp Act Crisis

A Tax on Paper The British also created new taxes to collect money from the colonists. In 1765, Parliament passed the Stamp Act. This law made colonists pay a tax on just about every kind of printed paper. The tax applied to about fifty different items in all.

The Big Question

Why did the Stamp Act cause so much anger in the colonies?

People began to protest against the Stamp Act.

Under the Stamp Act, colonists had to buy special tax stamps from a tax collector. They would put a stamp on each of the taxed items they used. Every time they bought such things as a newspaper, a calendar, a marriage license, or any kind of legal or business paper, they had to pay a tax. They even had to pay a tax on playing cards. This made many of the colonists *very* angry.

Do you see why the colonists were so outraged? Had their own colonial assemblies passed this tax law? No, they had not. It was the British Parliament in faraway London, England.

Sure, British subjects living in Great Britain were already paying a stamp tax. But those subjects were represented in Parliament. The colonists were not. They could not elect members of Parliament. They had no voice and no representatives in Parliament. What right did Parliament have to pass a law taxing them? None. Absolutely none. To the colonists, this was "**taxation without representation**." It was completely unjust!

Vocabulary

"taxation without representation," (phrase), the idea that American colonists did not have a say in the English Parliament, which enacted taxes without their consent

A Leader Emerges

One colonist who strongly protested the Stamp Act was a twenty-nine-year old Virginian named Patrick Henry. Patrick Henry was a member of the Virginia assembly, known as the Virginia House of Burgesses. He gave a powerful speech against the new tax. He warned that the Stamp Act would take away the colonists' liberty.

Patrick Henry spoke out against the Stamp Act.

Patrick Henry's speech was printed in newspapers throughout the colonies. The speech made people think. In New York, Boston, Newport, and other places throughout the colonies, people protested, debated, and formed groups called the Sons of Liberty. These groups threatened the stamp tax collectors. Many stamp tax collectors decided that the best thing to do was get out of town and forget about selling tax stamps.

The Colonies Protest

The Sons of Liberty did more than threaten tax collectors. They also organized a **boycott** of British goods. People

> **Vocabulary**
>
> **boycott,** n. a form of organized protest in which people refuse to buy goods or have anything to do with a particular group or country

throughout the colonies agreed not to buy goods from Great Britain as long as the Stamp Act remained a law.

Like the Sons of Liberty, women's groups called the Daughters of Liberty helped support the boycott. One of the most important goods purchased from British merchants was cloth. To make up for the growing shortage in the colonies, the Daughters of Liberty wove their own cloth.

Vocabulary

Patriot, n. a person who supported the cause of the colonists during the American Revolution

"course of action," (phrase), a plan to respond to a situation

The Sons of Liberty, Daughters of Liberty, and the many other people who supported the colonists' cause also gave themselves another name. They called themselves **Patriots**.

Colonial leaders knew they could do more to put pressure on Parliament. Colonial leaders called for a special meeting of all the colonies to decide on a **course of action**. In October 1765, nine colonies sent delegates, or representatives, to the meeting held

Patrick Henry's newspaper article influenced many people in the colonies.

in New York. Delegates at the Stamp Act Congress agreed on a number of statements that confirmed the rights of colonists as British subjects. They also asked Parliament to **repeal** the hated law.

These actions by the colonists shocked the leaders of the British government. They were especially worried by the meeting of the Stamp Act Congress. Never before had the colonies acted together against the British government. British leaders did not want this to become a habit. British merchants weren't happy either. The boycott was causing them to lose a lot of money.

Vocabulary

repeal, v. to cancel or do away with something, such as a law

resistance, n. an effort to stop a law or policy from taking effect

In 1766, after one year, Parliament repealed the Stamp Act. When the news reached America, the colonists celebrated. Through their **resistance**, they had brought an end to the hated Stamp Act. Of course, they still loved their king. No one was talking about leaving the British Empire. The Stamp Act had really been nothing more than a conflict between members of the same family.

Chapter 8
Parliament Stumbles Again

Who Is in Charge? You might think Parliament would get the message: no taxation without representation. The colonists had drawn the line there, but the British government still needed money, and it needed to show who was boss. And so in 1767—just one year after repealing the Stamp Act—Parliament tried again. This time, as part of the Townshend Acts, it placed taxes on glass, paint, lead, paper, and a number of other goods that colonists imported.

The Big Question

Why did the British government repeal the Townshend Acts?

The British government taxed imported goods that the colonists needed.

This was Parliament's thinking: the colonists need these goods, so when ships deliver them to colonial **harbors**, our officials will be there to collect the tax. Parliament made things worse by saying that whomever was arrested for not paying the tax would be tried without a jury.

> **Vocabulary**
>
> **harbor,** n. a part of a body of water that is next to land and provides a safe place for ships to anchor
>
> **manufacturer,** n. a person or company that makes or produces an item to be sold

Taxation without representation again? And this time, trial without a jury? So much for the "rights of Englishmen"! Once again, the Sons of Liberty swung into action. They organized another boycott of all British goods. This boycott was as successful as the first one. The colonists didn't stop at making their own cloth. They also made their own paint, lead, glass, and paper. The quality of the homemade items was not as good as those purchased from Britain, and it may have cost more to make them, but the colonists would make do to get their point across!

The boycott lasted for nearly three years. Once again, the colonists succeeded. British merchants and **manufacturers** lost so much money because of the boycott that they demanded that Parliament repeal the new taxes.

It was one thing for the colonists to demand that Parliament repeal a tax. Parliament could ignore them if it wished. But Parliament could hardly ignore the powerful businessmen of their own country.

So in 1770, Parliament repealed all but one of the taxes. The British government kept the tax on tea as a symbol of their right to pass laws *and* tax the colonies. The colonists responded accordingly. They ended their boycott of all goods from Britain, except for one. Can you guess which item they continued to boycott?

Parliament had left the tax on tea to show that it had the right to tax the colonists. The colonists continued the boycott on tea to show that Parliament did not have the right to tax them. Each side was willing to leave it at that for the time being. The colonists, who were big tea drinkers, didn't give up tea completely. They simply bought their tea from Dutch merchants who smuggled it into the colonies.

The Boston Massacre

Meanwhile, more British troops arrived in the colonies. The colonists grew alarmed. For them, the presence of British soldiers represented a threat to their freedom. The British said the soldiers were needed to defend the colonists against Native American attacks. If that were true, then why weren't the soldiers on the frontier, where the Native Americans were? Why were so many troops located in eastern cities, like Philadelphia, New York, and Boston? In Boston in particular, troops seemed to be everywhere—on the street corners, in front of buildings, in the parks.

The citizens of Boston jeered at the soldiers. They made fun of them. They tried to make their lives miserable. Because British soldiers sometimes had regular jobs, tensions grew over employment opportunities, too. In several cities, fights broke out between colonists and soldiers.

Those fights were not nearly as bad, though, as what happened in Boston on the evening of March 5, 1770. There, a crowd of men and boys gathered around a lone British soldier on guard duty. They shouted insults and threw snowballs at him. Some of the snowballs had rocks inside of them.

The frightened soldier called for help. More British soldiers arrived. The crowd grew larger. The shouts, the dares, and the insults grew louder and angrier.

Then, for reasons that are unclear, the soldiers turned their guns on the angry crowd and shot. When the smoke cleared, five colonists lay dead or wounded. Their blood stained the snow-covered street. One of them was Crispus Attucks, who had once been enslaved and now worked as a sailor. Crispus Attucks

Crispus Attucks was the first African American to die for the Patriot cause.

was the first African American to die for the cause of American liberty. He was not the last.

A few days later, more than half of the population of Boston turned out for a funeral march for the dead men. Shops were closed. Church bells rang. Angry Bostonians called the killing a ***massacre***—a needless killing of defenseless people. The event became known as the Boston Massacre.

> **Vocabulary**
>
> **massacre,** n. the violent killing of defenseless people
>
> **silversmith,** n. a person who makes things out of silver
>
> **engraving,** n. a design or pattern that is cut into the surface of an object

A Boston **silversmith** named Paul Revere made a copper **engraving** that showed soldiers firing on a group of perfectly peaceful, innocent citizens. Many paper copies can be printed from a single engraving. That is exactly what Revere did.

No one knows for sure whether Revere actually saw the shooting. Some of the things shown in the engraving are not true. But Paul Revere was a Son of Liberty. He made that engraving because he wanted to make people angry at the British. Sure, the citizens who were shot had been asking for trouble. But they certainly did not deserve to die.

The British soldiers who fired on the crowd were tried by a local court. It found six soldiers innocent and two guilty of manslaughter. The lawyer who defended them was John Adams.

Chapter 9
A Change in Thinking

Calm Before the Storm In time, the anger over the Boston Massacre died down. The British government didn't do anything new to upset the American colonists. For the most part, American colonists tried not to upset the British government. Therefore the next three years were mostly calm.

> **The Big Question**
>
> What was the Committee of Correspondence?

In the early 1770s, colonists' feelings toward London and Britain itself were changing.

Still, the way many colonists thought about Britain was changing. A country that sets up colonies in other lands is often called the *mother country*. That's what most colonists had always called England, or Britain. Even those who had never been there called Britain home.

The British described their relationship with the colonies the same way. Prime Minister William Pitt once said, "This is the mother country, they are the children. They must obey, and we prescribe [set the rules]."

But children grow up. They learn to do things for themselves. They gain confidence. They need to do things their own way. Eventually, they live on their own. Independently.

After the Boston Massacre, some colonists wondered whether that time had come. This change in thinking happened slowly. At first only a few felt that way. Most colonists wanted to stay in the British Empire. They were loyal to their king. They just thought it was time for the British government to stop making rules for them.

A small number of colonists talked about going further. They believed that they could only keep their liberties by breaking away from Britain. The colonies, they believed, must become independent.

Sam Adams

Sam Adams of Boston was one of the colonists who believed in independence. Adams came from an important Boston family.

Sam Adams wanted the colonies to be independent of Great Britain.

In 1765, at the time of the Stamp Act, Adams helped to organize the Sons of Liberty. He was one of the leaders in the boycotts against British goods.

From that time forward, Adams worked to convince others that it was time to separate from Great Britain. In newspaper articles he told colonists to stand up against Britain for their rights. "The liberties of our country . . . are worth defending at all risks," he wrote. It would be a "disgrace" to allow our freedoms to be taken away "from us by violence, without a struggle, or be cheated out of them by tricks . . ."

After the Boston Massacre, Adams and others in Boston created a way to alert colonists if (or when) the British government threatened their liberties again. In 1772, they set up a **Committee** of Correspondence.

Vocabulary

committee, n. a group of people selected to do a certain task

quill pen, n. a pen made from the feather of a bird

Correspondence means "an exchange of letters." If the British again took away any "rights of Englishmen," committee members would immediately send letters across Massachusetts with the news.

The idea spread quickly to other colonies. Soon there was a great network of Committees of Correspondence. They could get news out quickly within each colony and from one colony to another.

Of course these committees didn't put away their **quill pens** and paper and wait for the next conflict. They wrote to each other often. Little by little, the idea of independence spread throughout the colonies. Those who wanted independence were still in the minority. But what would happen if the British government threatened their liberties once again?

Rising Tensions

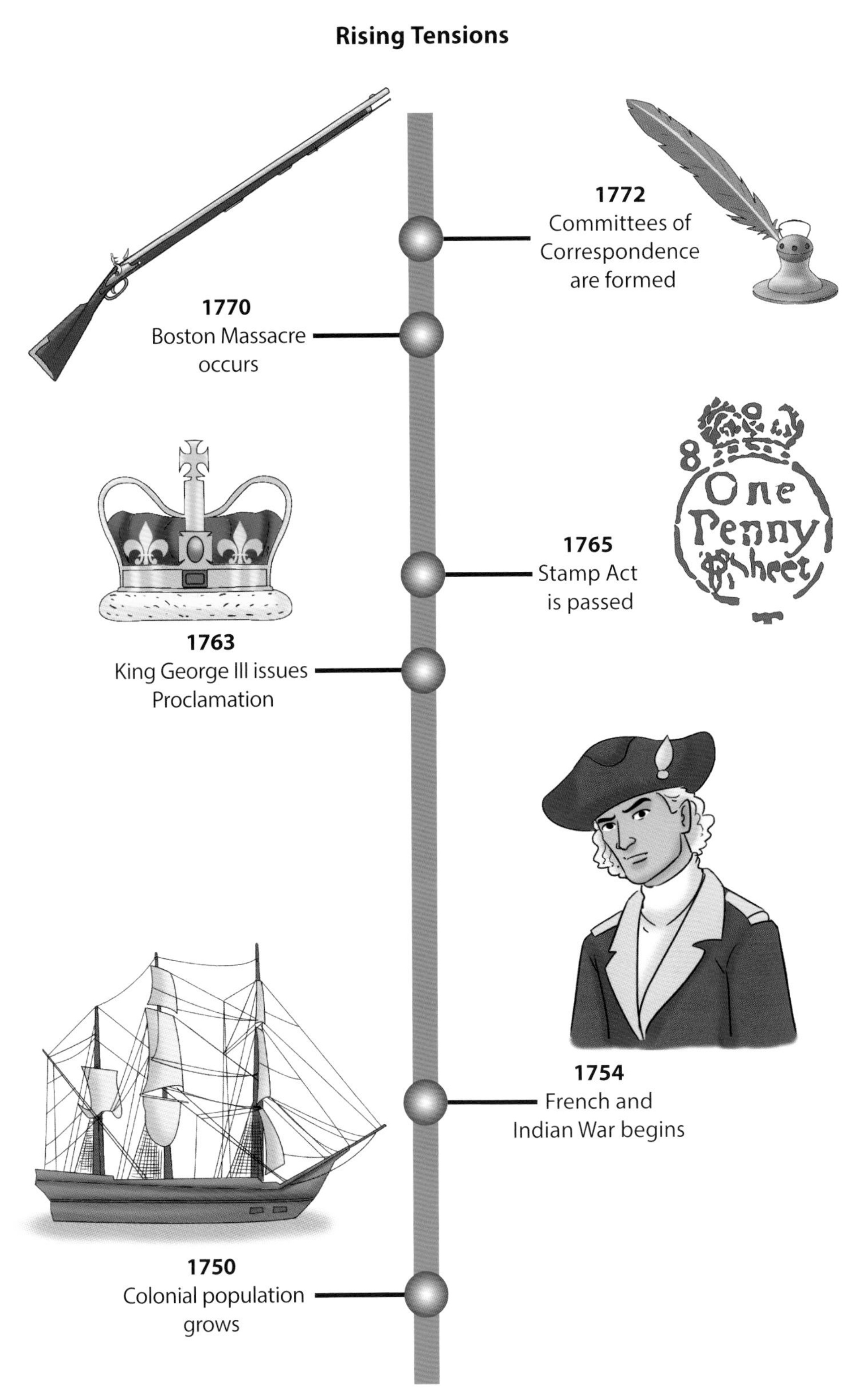

Over time, relations became strained between Great Britain and the colonies.

Chapter 10
A Tea Party in Boston

> **The Big Question**
>
> What were the events that led to the Boston Tea Party?

Parliament Makes Another Mistake Have you ever heard the expression, "He was too clever for his own good"? It means that sometimes a person thinks he has a smart solution to a problem. Instead, his solution makes things worse.

Few sayings better describe what the British government did next. Parliament had left the tax on tea just to show the colonists that it had the right to tax them. Meanwhile the colonists had maintained the boycott on tea just to show Parliament that it didn't.

Parliament decided its plan had not worked. British tea merchants had lost their colonial customers. The colonists were buying tea smuggled in by Dutch merchants. As a result, the government hadn't collected more than a few pennies in taxes. So in 1773, Parliament came up with another plan. It passed the Tea Act.

Parliament's new plan was clever but tricky. Parliament lowered the price of the tea itself. But it also kept the tax on the tea. When the new price of the tea was added to the tax, the total cost was less than what the colonists paid for tea from the Dutch.

Tea was a popular drink in the colonies.

Parliament thought the colonists would now buy British tea again. When they did, they would be paying the tea tax! Soon two thousand chests of tea were loaded aboard British ships bound for the American colonies. Once there, the tea would be sold by certain colonial merchants.

Unfortunately, Parliament was "too clever for its own good." The Tea Act of 1773 showed how poorly Parliament understood the colonists. The colonists did not care about the price of tea. They cared about "taxation without representation." They were *not* going to pay that tea tax, no matter what British tea cost.

News Travels Fast

As British tea ships headed for the colonies, Committees of Correspondence went to work. The news spread through the colonies. The Sons of Liberty prevented the tea ships from being unloaded in several ports. In Philadelphia, for example, the Sons of Liberty sent a letter to the captain of a ship waiting in the harbor to unload its chests of tea. "I wouldn't try to land that tea if I were you," said the letter. "Your ship may just happen to be set on fire . . ." The captain got the idea and decided not to dock.

Colonists in other colonial port cities responded the same way. Some captains had their ships wait in the harbor. Others turned their ships around and headed home. That is not what happened in Boston.

Time for Tea

Early in December 1773, three tea ships entered Boston Harbor. Citizens gathered at a town meeting. They demanded that the

No one was fooled by the costumes worn by the colonists when they tossed the tea into Boston Harbor.

governor of the colony order the ships to leave. The governor did not like Sam Adams or the Sons of Liberty. He refused.

Colonists took matters into their own hands. On the night of December 16, 1773, a group of colonists dressed as Native Americans as a symbol of independence. Then they rowed out to the ships in the harbor. They boarded the ships and dumped every chest of tea into the water. Exactly 342 chests went into the harbor. All of this was done in a quiet, businesslike way. When they were through, the "Native Americans" swept the deck and put everything back in its proper place. This event became known as the Boston Tea Party.

The Intolerable Acts

When Parliament and the king heard about the Boston Tea Party, they were outraged. Parliament passed laws to punish the people of Boston and the whole Massachusetts colony. One law closed the Port of Boston until the colonists paid for the wasted tea. For a city that depended on trading and fishing, this was a harsh punishment. Parliament hoped that Boston's merchants and fishermen would turn in the guilty persons. Maybe they would even pay for the tea themselves. They did neither.

A second law took away most of the Massachusetts colony's self-government. The British also appointed an army general to be the governor of Massachusetts. The new governor came with thousands of British soldiers. The Quartering Act forced the colonists to house and feed the soldiers.

These laws became known as the **Intolerable** Acts because the colonists would not tolerate or accept them.

Vocabulary

intolerable, adj. unbearable

oppose, v. to be against something

Making Enemies

The British government failed to understand the effects of its actions. The new laws caused it to lose friends and make enemies. Even colonists who were loyal to Britain, who **opposed** the Sons of Liberty, who wanted to buy British tea and pay the tea tax felt the new laws were too harsh.

Tax collectors were unpopular. This tax collector has been painted with melted tar and covered with feathers.

Once again, the Committees of Correspondence spread the news. The colonies decided to stand with the people of Boston to **resist** the Intolerable Acts.

> **Vocabulary**
>
> **resist,** v. to go against

Chapter 11
The Colonies Resist

Help from Other Colonies

Parliament was right about one thing: the Intolerable Acts made the people of Boston and the rest of Massachusetts suffer. However, Parliament didn't expect the other colonies to come to their aid.

The Big Question

How did colonists' attitudes and view of themselves begin to change?

Pennsylvania sent barrels of flour to the people of Massachusetts. New York sent sheep. South Carolina sent sacks of rice. Connecticut sent money. Virginia sent corn and wheat.

Virginia's leaders even went a step further. They set aside a day of fasting and prayer for the people of Boston. They also declared that the Intolerable Acts were a threat to liberty in every colony. If the king and Parliament could do these things to Massachusetts, what would stop them from doing the same to other colonies?

Throughout the colonies, there was a determination to help the people of Boston.

The Virginians took a bold step. They called for delegates from all of the colonies to meet and discuss what to do next. This would be the second time delegates met to resist an act of Parliament. The first time, the Stamp Act Congress, had been successful. This time, though, the British government seemed determined not to back down.

The First Continental Congress

In September 1774, fifty-six colonial leaders met in Philadelphia. They represented twelve of the thirteen British colonies in North America. Only Georgia did not send delegates. The colonists thought this meeting was important. We can tell by the delegates they chose. George Washington, Patrick Henry, and Thomas Jefferson represented Virginia. Sam Adams and his cousin John represented Massachusetts. New York sent John Jay. Jay later served on the **Supreme Court** of the United States. John Adams wrote in his diary, "There is in the Congress a collection of the greatest men upon this continent."

Vocabulary

Supreme Court, n. the highest court in the land

declaration, n. a formal statement

This meeting became known as the First Continental Congress. The delegates discussed their common problems. They shared their anger at the British government. They issued a **Declaration** of Rights. The declaration said that as British colonists, they were entitled to all the "rights of Englishmen." They listed the ways Parliament had taken their rights away since the French and Indian War. They also told King George III that the colonists were still loyal to him. They asked him to consider their complaints.

George Washington (left) and Thomas Jefferson (right) attended the First Continental Congress.

The First Continental Congress did two more things. It voted to stop all trade with the British until Parliament repealed the Intolerable Acts. Until Parliament removed the laws, colonists would buy nothing from Britain and sell nothing to Britain. The Congress also agreed to meet again in May 1775 if Parliament still had not given back their rights.

A New Identity

The First Continental Congress and the Declaration of Rights were the most **defiant** actions the colonies had ever taken. But something more than defiance had happened. This "something" had no exact name. There is no exact date when it started. Still, it was as important as any of the **resolutions** passed by the First Continental Congress. Maybe it started with those shipments of flour and rice and money to Boston from the other colonies. Maybe it began with the Stamp Act Congress. Maybe it had been happening all

Vocabulary

defiant, adj. breaking the rules on purpose

resolution, n. a final decision usually meant to solve a problem or create a course of action

along, before anyone was aware of it. That "something" was that the colonies were coming together as never before.

Before this, each colony had thought of itself as separate from the others. The colonists thought of themselves as Virginians or New Yorkers or Georgians. When they thought of an attachment to any other place, it was to Great Britain. That was partly because each colony had more to do with Britain than it did with other colonies. It was also due to the fact that the colonists thought of themselves as British citizens, with all the "rights of Englishmen."

The colonists began to think of themselves as Americans, not as members of thirteen separate colonies.

By the end of the First Continental Congress, many colonists were thinking of themselves as part of one country, not as people living in thirteen different ones. They were more aware of the things they had in common. They were more aware that they needed each other. Patrick Henry summed up the new awareness perfectly. He told the First Continental Congress, "The distinctions [differences] between Virginians, Pennsylvanians, New Yorkers, and New Englanders, are no more. I am not a Virginian but an American."

Chapter 12
The Fighting Begins

Maybe This and Maybe That

Maybe if King George III had paid attention to the colonists' pleas . . .

> **The Big Question**
>
> What was Patrick Henry's point of view?

Maybe if the British government had taken its troops out of the colonies . . .

Maybe if many things had happened, war might have been prevented.

Or maybe not. Maybe by that time, the colonists had gone too far down the road toward independence to turn back. No one knows for sure what *might* have happened.

We do know what *did* happen. By the start of 1775, more and more colonists expected the quarrels with the mother country to lead to war. By spring, the militias in many colonies were preparing to fight. Each militia was made up of citizens who volunteered to be part-time soldiers.

In March, members of the Virginia General Assembly debated whether their colony should prepare for war as well. Some opposed the idea, but Patrick Henry believed the time had come for action. Everyone at the meeting knew Henry was a great speaker.

Patrick Henry was a very persuasive speaker. Virginians responded to Patrick Henry's "give me liberty or give me death!" speech.

When he stood to address the members, a hush fell over the room. Some of the earlier speakers had said that maybe Britain would still change its mind. Patrick Henry responded:

> **Vocabulary**
>
> **brethren,** n. members of the same group or family

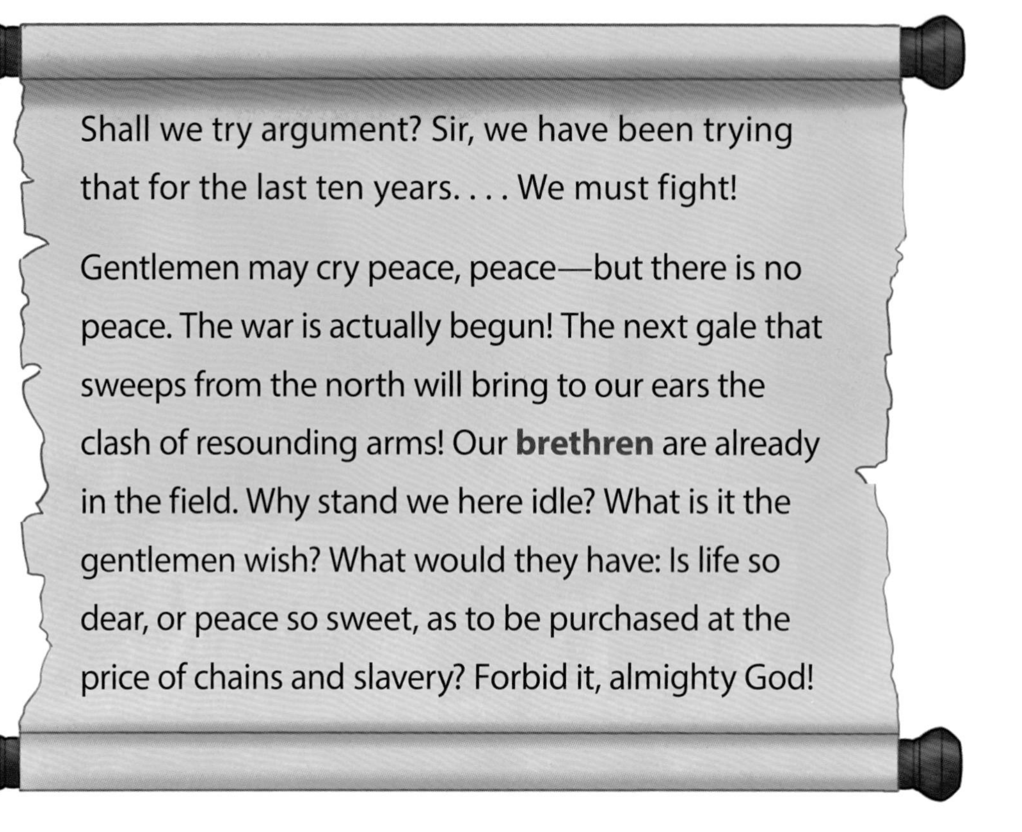

Shall we try argument? Sir, we have been trying that for the last ten years. . . . We must fight!

Gentlemen may cry peace, peace—but there is no peace. The war is actually begun! The next gale that sweeps from the north will bring to our ears the clash of resounding arms! Our **brethren** are already in the field. Why stand we here idle? What is it the gentlemen wish? What would they have: Is life so dear, or peace so sweet, as to be purchased at the price of chains and slavery? Forbid it, almighty God!

Then Patrick Henry stood tall. He raised his arms high. His voice clear as a bell, he finished with the words that have stirred lovers of liberty ever since:

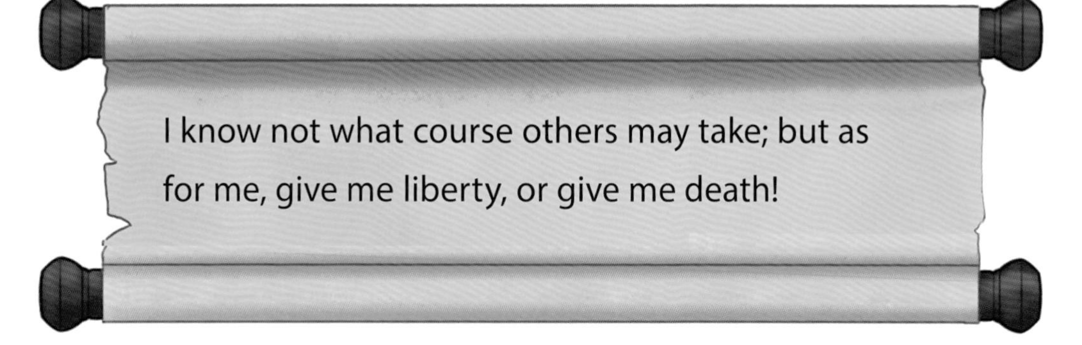

I know not what course others may take; but as for me, give me liberty, or give me death!

Patrick Henry was wrong when he said that the war had begun. Three weeks after his speech, the real fighting began. For several months, militias in Massachusetts had been training to fight. These farmers and townspeople called themselves **Minutemen** because they could be ready to fight on a minute's notice. To prepare for battle, the Minutemen had been collecting guns, gunpowder, and other supplies. They hid these supplies in the village of Concord, about fifteen miles northwest of Boston.

> **Vocabulary**
>
> **Minutemen,** n. people who volunteered to serve in the American militia and were ready to fight at a moment's notice

Remember that the British sent an army general to serve as the governor of Massachusetts? The new governor was General Thomas Gage. General Gage learned about those hidden supplies in Concord. He also learned that two Sons of Liberty, Sam Adams and John Hancock, were hiding in the town of Lexington.

Lexington was on the way to Concord. General Gage figured he could **kill two birds with one stone**. He would send his soldiers to Lexington first to capture Adams and Hancock. The soldiers would then continue on to Concord and take the Minutemen's hidden supplies.

> **Vocabulary**
>
> **"kill two birds with one stone,"** (idiom), to accomplish two different things at the same time

General Gage planned for his soldiers to leave Boston in the dead of night. That way no one would notice. They could take Lexington by surprise. But the Sons of Liberty found out about his plan. Two Sons of Liberty, Paul Revere and William Dawes, got ready to ride ahead of the British soldiers and warn citizens along the way.

Paul Revere's Ride

There were two routes to Lexington. Which one would the **redcoats** take? The first route was longer, but it was entirely over land. The shorter route required that the troops first cross the Charles River by rowboat before starting their overland march.

> **Vocabulary**
>
> **redcoat,** n. a nickname given to British soldiers because of the color of their uniforms

William Dawes started out along the long route to Lexington. As he went, he called out to Patriot homes that the redcoats were on their way.

Paul Revere hung back, in case the British decided to cross the Charles River. He had already arranged for a young man to signal to the Sons of Liberty waiting on the opposite shore. From the tower of the Old North Church in Boston, the young man would hang one lantern if the British were traveling by land. He would hang two lanterns if they were traveling by water.

When Paul Revere realized the British were planning to row across the river, he passed along the information to the signaler. That night, two lanterns burned brightly in the tower of the Old North Church. The British would be coming by water!

Paul Revere and two friends hurried to a hidden rowboat. They rowed across the water ahead of the British troops. Once on shore, Revere borrowed a horse from another Son of Liberty. He then galloped off to carry the warning to Lexington and Concord.

Paul Revere warned colonists that the British were on the way.

Stopping at every village and farm, he pounded on doors and sounded the alarm. Many people believe that Paul Revere shouted, "The British are coming!" or "The redcoats are coming!" It is more likely, though, that his warning cry was, "The Regulars are coming!" A *Regular* was another name for a British soldier. Revere never made it to Concord, but he was able to warn Sam Adams and John Hancock in Lexington. The two men escaped before the British arrived.

The Battle at Lexington

British troops arrived in Lexington at dawn, expecting to see no one. Instead, they saw seventy Minutemen facing them on the **village green**. The leader of the Minutemen, Captain John Parker, told his

> **Vocabulary**
>
> **"village green,"** (phrase), an open grassy area in a village or town

men, "Stand your ground. Don't fire unless fired upon." Then he added, "But if they mean to have war, let it begin here."

There they stood. On the one side were six hundred to seven hundred well-trained, well-armed soldiers in handsome uniforms; on the other was a much smaller group in rough dress and with fewer weapons. The British officer ordered the Minutemen to leave.

Suddenly, someone opened fire. Both sides started shooting. Within minutes, eight Minutemen were dead. Another ten lay wounded.

The British caught both William Dawes and Paul Revere before they could get to Concord. However, another Patriot named Dr. Samuel Prescott rode off with the warning of a British attack.

The British troops next pushed on to Concord. They expected to find the hidden **stockpile** of weapons. However, the colonists had moved most of their supplies. This did not stop the British from destroying what little they did find.

Vocabulary

stockpile, n. a large amount of something being stored for future use

unfurl, v. to unroll and spread out like a piece of fabric or a flag

By the rude bridge that arched the flood,
Their flag to April's breeze ***unfurled,***
Here once the embattled farmers stood,
And fired the shot heard round the world.

Concord Hymn

Many years later, Ralph Waldo Emerson wrote a poem to be read at a memorial ceremony celebrating the Battle of Concord. This is the first stanza.

Once again, the British were surprised to find Minutemen waiting for them. This time there were nearly four hundred of them gathered at the North Bridge, near the Concord village green.

Soldiers at the bridge opened fire. Minutemen fired back. After five minutes of fighting, the British decided to return to Boston.

That long march back to Boston became a nightmare for the British soldiers. Paul Revere had alerted all of the people living along the route. They had watched the British march toward Lexington in the early morning hours. Now they waited behind stone fences, barns, and trees for the British to return. In their bright red uniforms, the soldiers were easy targets. Shots rang out all along the route. Before the British got back to Boston that night, the Minutemen killed seventy-three soldiers and wounded another two hundred. That was nearly half of the number of soldiers who had set out for Lexington and Concord earlier that day. The colonists suffered losses too—nearly fifty men died. The Americans did not know it at the time, but the War for Independence had officially begun.

Chapter 13
Preparing for War

May 10, 1775 Once again the leading men from every American colony gathered in Philadelphia for a Continental Congress. This time, though, was different. This time, there had been fighting. This time, men had died.

The Big Question

Why was George Washington chosen to be the leader of the Continental Army?

Most of the delegates to the Second Continental Congress weren't sure what to do next. They hated the thought of separating from Great Britain and their king. Couldn't the Continental Congress try again to solve their issues with the mother country? At the same time, they could not ignore the fact that fighting had started. Shouldn't they prepare for more fighting, just in case?

Vocabulary

petition, n. a formal written request for change signed by several people

policy, n. an official course of action

The Second Continental Congress did both. Delegates wrote a **petition** to King George III. A petition is like a request. They told the king they were still loyal to him. There was no talk of independence. They said they didn't want to break up the British Empire. They only asked the king to make his government change its bad **policies** and restore the colonists' rights.

The colonists' petition is delivered to King George III.

At the same time, the Congress prepared for more fighting. John Adams of Massachusetts took the lead. Adams believed that the local militias were fine for fighting here and there. To fight a war, though, they needed to create a real American army—an "Army of the United Colonies."

At the time, members of the Massachusetts militia were camped outside of Boston, near the British troops. Those militiamen, said Adams, were ready to be the first soldiers in the new army.

But who would lead Adams's "Army of the United Colonies"? How fortunate the Congress was, Adams continued, to have the right man for the job in that very room! He was a man of "great talents and excellent character." He was an experienced military leader from Virginia. As Adams continued to speak, all eyes turned to the tall man dressed in an old militia uniform, standing in the back of the room. The man quickly turned and walked out. He wanted the delegates to be free to discuss him without him being present. That man was George Washington.

George Washington was chosen to lead the Continental Army.

Adams was right, and the other delegates agreed. Washington was the perfect man to lead the Continental Army, as it came to be called. He had gained his military experience in the French and Indian War. After that, he returned to Mount Vernon, Virginia, to run his plantation. He was a member of the Virginia House of Burgesses and a supporter of the Patriot cause. He was also among the best-known and wealthiest men in the colonies. Everyone admired him for his devotion to duty, his cool head, and strong will.

It was settled. Washington would command the Continental Army, and its first troops would be the Massachusetts militiamen camped around Boston. They might be needed for action soon. More British soldiers were arriving in the colonies.

Washington headed to Massachusetts to take charge of the militia. Before his arrival, though, the American soldiers fought an important battle near Boston.

On July 3, 1775, George Washington took command of the Continental Army.

Two hills overlook the city of Boston: Bunker Hill and Breed's Hill. Every general knows that it's a great advantage to control the high ground. From the top of a hill, you can fire down at the enemy below—especially if you have cannons. Meanwhile, the enemy has to fight its way uphill. The British understood this idea, but they were not very worried about the untrained Massachusetts militiamen. They did not bother to guard the two hills. On the night of June 16, 1775, the militia suddenly marched to Breed's Hill and climbed it. They were supposed to take up positions on Bunker Hill, but moved onto the wrong hill.

All night they dug **trenches**, piling the earth into walls six feet high for their protection. When the morning came, the British were surprised to see the colonial militia in control of the hill.

Vocabulary

trench, n. a narrow ditch dug into the ground

ammunition, n. bullets or shells

General Gage was now worried that the militia would be able to fire on his troops below. They could even use cannons to fire upon the British ships in the harbor. Gage needed to drive the militia off the hill. Gage didn't know that the Massachusetts militia didn't have any cannons.

The next day, British soldiers marched up Breed's Hill. The colonists had only a small amount of **ammunition**. They couldn't afford to waste any. They stood shoulder to shoulder behind their earthen walls. When the British got close, the militiamen opened fire. Hundreds of redcoats fell. The rest fled back down the hill.

Once more the British marched up the hill. Once more they were driven back by a hail of bullets. After the second charge, the colonists began to run out of ammunition. When the British marched up the hill a third time, the militia retreated.

Bunker Hill proved to be a very costly victory for the British.

The British won the hill but at a terrible cost. More than a thousand soldiers were killed or wounded. Just as during their march back from Concord, the British lost about half their men. A British officer said that his army couldn't stand many more "victories" like this. Even though the battle took place on Breed's Hill, it is known as the Battle of Bunker Hill. The Battle of Bunker Hill was very important to the colonists. They lost the hill, but they won new confidence. They were beginning to believe these citizen-soldiers could hold their own against one of the world's greatest armies—the British army.

Soon after, the colonists learned King George III's answer to their petition. He had no intention of backing down. Instead, he was eager for a fight.

Chapter 14
The Great Declaration

> **The Big Question**
>
> What was the Declaration of Independence?

Coming to a Decision By the start of 1776, the argument with Great Britain had lasted more than ten years. The fighting had gone on for almost one. Still, many colonists weren't sure whether they really wanted independence.

> **Vocabulary**
>
> **Loyalist,** n. a person living in the colonies who did not support the American cause and remained loyal to Great Britain

A number of colonists opposed independence. These people were called **Loyalists**. Loyalists belonged to different religions and came from different social classes. They had different reasons for their loyalty. Some Loyalists made their decision for economic reasons. Some chose the British side for political reasons. Others followed religious or personal values. But all Loyalists agreed on one thing: the need to stay faithful to the king and to Great Britain.

No colony had ever broken away from a mother country. Giving up a place in the world's greatest empire and all the advantages of being part of it—was that really a smart idea? On the other hand, Patriots

PLAIN TRUTH;

ADDRESSED TO THE

INHABITANTS

OF

AMERICA,

Containing, Remarks

ON A LATE PAMPHLET,

entitled

COMMON SENSE:

Wherein are shewn, that the Scheme of INDEPENDENCE is Ruinous, Delusive, and Impracticable: That were the Author's Asseverations, Respecting the Power of AMERICA, as Real as Nugatory; Reconciliation on liberal Principles with GREAT BRITAIN, would be exalted Policy: And that circumstanced as we are, Permanent Liberty, and True Happiness, can only be obtained, by HONORABLE CONNECTIONS, with that Kingdom.

WRITTEN BY CANDIDUS.

Will ye turn from flattery, and attend to this Side.?

There TRUTH, unlicenc'd, walks; and dares accost
Even Kings themselves, the Monarchs of the Free!

THOMSON on the Liberties of BRITAIN.

PHILADELPHIA:
Printed, and Sold, by R. BELL, in Third-Street.

MDCCLXXVI.

Thomas Paine, a twenty-nine-year-old English immigrant, helped to persuade many colonists that the time for independence had arrived.

argued, shouldn't the colonists defend their rights and liberties? It was a very tough decision.

The decision became easier after Thomas Paine wrote a **pamphlet** called *Common Sense*. Paine had a great and rare skill. He could write about important ideas in everyday language. If you could read at all, you could understand *Common Sense*. Paine's pamphlet was read throughout the colonies. People talked about it in their homes, on street corners, and in taverns and inns.

> **Vocabulary**
>
> **pamphlet,** n. a small booklet that includes information or ideas about a single topic

A lot of what Paine wrote was, in fact, plain common sense. He got readers to think about his ideas not just by telling them what he thought but also by asking what *they* thought. Did it make any sense for America to be ruled by a small nation three thousand miles away? Did it make sense for people to be ruled by one man, a king, just because he was born into a certain family? Wouldn't it be better if the colonists chose their own rulers?

Paine said that it was common sense for Americans to cut all ties to Great Britain. It was common sense for Americans to be independent and create a government of their own. Americans didn't need a king. They could live in a land where "the law is king." The more they thought about it, the more Americans agreed. They didn't need the Parliament and the king to rule them. They had plenty of experience in choosing their own leaders and ruling themselves. Perhaps it really was time, then, to separate and go their own way.

The Declaration of Independence

In June 1776, the Second Continental Congress took up the question of independence. Congress agreed that the time had come to separate from Great Britain. The Congress chose a committee to write a declaration, or statement. The purpose

IN CONGRESS, JULY 4, 1776.

The unanimous Declaration of the thirteen united States of America,

The Declaration of Independence formally announced the colonists' separation from Great Britain.

of the declaration was to explain why the colonies were breaking away from Great Britain.

The committee chosen to write the declaration included John Adams, Benjamin Franklin, and Thomas Jefferson. Which committee member should do the main writing? Benjamin Franklin and George Washington were probably the two most famous Americans alive. John Adams was one of the first leaders to speak out in favor of independence. Thomas Jefferson, however, was known as a fine writer. Franklin and Adams chose him to write the declaration.

What Jefferson produced became the most famous document not only in American history, but also in the history of the entire world. Jefferson wanted the world to know all the bad things this king had done and all the rights he had taken away. So he listed each of them. He also explained why the king's actions made it right for the colonists to break away from Britain.

Vocabulary

endow, v. to give someone something valuable

We hold these truths to be self-evident, that all men are created equal, that they are ***endowed*** *by their Creator with certain unalienable rights, that among these are life, liberty, and the pursuit of happiness.*

Jefferson also stated, *"That to secure these rights, governments are* ***instituted*** *[created] . . ."* In other words, the reason we have governments is to protect our rights.

Vocabulary

institute, v. to establish or start something

revolution, n. the act of overthrowing a government with the hopes of starting a new and different one

What if a government doesn't protect those rights? What if it takes them away? Then, said Jefferson, people have the right to create new governments for themselves. That's what the people of the thirteen colonies were now doing.

On July 4, 1776, Congress adopted this Declaration of Independence. On that day the American colonies became independent states. Together, they made up the United States of America. Today, Americans celebrate July 4th as their Independence Day.

During the next month, in towns and cities across the states, crowds gathered to hear the Declaration of Independence read aloud. Everywhere in the new United States of America, church bells rang out. Soldiers fired cannons and shot off guns. Citizens lit great bonfires in celebration.

Meanwhile, back in Philadelphia, the delegates to the Second Continental Congress were more serious. The fifty-six men who signed the Declaration knew that if their **revolution** failed, the king would probably put them to death. Benjamin Franklin explained the need for all of the new states to work together. "Gentlemen," he said, "we must all hang together, [or] else we shall all hang separately."

Chapter 15
A Discouraging Start

Patriot Problems When you look at some of the problems the Americans faced, you can see that their chances of winning a war against Great Britain were not that great.

The Big Question

What challenges did George Washington face when raising an army?

For one thing, the thirteen new states may have been united against Great Britain, but their people certainly were not. While some Loyalists stayed quiet, others helped the British. Some wrote letters of support for the British cause. Some worked as spies. About fifty thousand Loyalists actually fought in the war on the side of Great Britain. Many of them moved to Great Britain or Canada after the Revolution.

Great Britain had one of the largest armies in the world. In addition to having fifty thousand Loyalist soldiers, the British hired about thirty thousand professional soldiers from other countries. Soldiers for hire are called **mercenaries**. Counting the mercenaries, Great Britain's army was five times larger than the Continental army. The British could also count on their Native American allies in the West.

Vocabulary

mercenary, n. a soldier from one country paid to fight for another country

The British army had many more trained soldiers than the Continental Army.

The British soldiers were well-trained fighters. Commanders could count on having their soldiers for a certain number of years. They had time to train their soldiers for battle.

General Washington had to build an army from scratch. His army was made up mainly of farmers, not professional soldiers.

Washington also never knew how many soldiers he could count on at any one time. Some joined the Continental army for a three-year term. Most volunteered to serve for less than a year. Some signed up for only three months. Others joined the Continental Army when the fighting got near their villages or farms. Then they would leave the army once the British troops moved on. Soldiers would often return to their farms at planting and harvesting time. With all these comings and goings, training an army was nearly impossible.

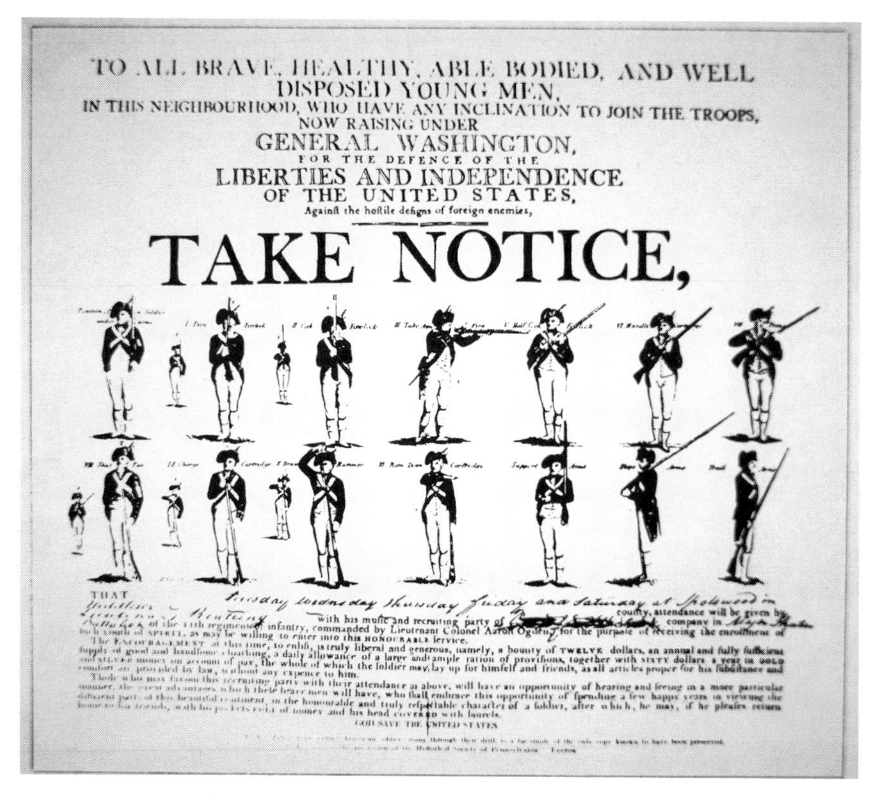

Posters like this one were used to find soldiers for the Continental Army.

Most soldiers in the Continental Army were farmers who volunteered to fight.

In addition to having a powerful army, Great Britain was one of the wealthiest nations in the world. The British could supply their army with whatever it needed. The Continental army was often short on cannons, gunpowder, food, and other supplies. It didn't even have enough uniforms. Throughout the war, most American soldiers fought in their own clothes. Several times during the war, General Washington wrote to the Continental Congress. If it didn't come up with money for supplies and pay the soldiers soon, "the army must absolutely break up."

As for a navy, the British had the greatest in the world. They had a hundred times as many warships as the Americans had.

None of that looked very good for the Americans.

The Americans did have a few things going for them, though. For one, they were fighting on their own land. Fresh soldiers and supplies were often available nearby. The British had to ship everything—including soldiers—from three thousand miles away. The Americans were also fighting to defend their homes, families, and freedom. Many soldiers on the British side were just fighting for money. That made a difference.

The size of the country was another advantage for the American side. If the British won in one part of the country, American armies could move to another. Thomas Paine wrote that the American plan would be like a game of checkers: "We can move out of *one* square to let you come in," he said to the British, "in order that we may afterwards take two or three for one." Since the Americans could keep moving around, he said, "we can always prevent a total defeat."

Support from Women and African Americans

The British could count on its professional soldiers, mercenaries, and Loyalists—including African Americans. In fact, most African Americans at this time supported the British cause. The British actively sought help from the African American community. They promised freedom to any enslaved person who fought for the king.

Women played an important part in supporting the Patriot cause.

The Patriots had their own sources of help. The Patriot side also had support from African Americans. It had important support from women, too.

Women played many roles in the American Revolution. Working in army camps, they washed, cooked, sewed, made gunpowder, and nursed the wounded. Sometimes women went into battle, even though they weren't supposed to. In one battle, Mary Ludwig Hays brought her husband's cannon crew water from a nearby stream. Pitcher carriers brought water to cool off the cannons, which would overheat in battle. She carried so many pitchers that they called her Molly Pitcher.

According to legend, Molly's husband became ill during the battle. The other members of his cannon crew had been killed. Molly loaded and fired the cannon by herself until other soldiers arrived to take over.

Another woman who helped the Patriot cause was Deborah Sampson. Sampson dressed in men's clothing and joined the army. She was a talented soldier. It was only when she was wounded that doctors found out she was a woman. A number of other women served as messengers and spies.

Of course, women didn't have to be on a battlefield to help the Patriot cause. One of their greatest contributions was at home. In addition to doing their usual work, they also did the work of the men who had gone off to fight. There were many women who kept the family farm going or the family business running.

As you have learned, in addition to women, African Americans also played a role in the American Revolution. About five thousand African Americans fought on the American side of the Revolutionary War. Most of them were free men from the northern states. They took part in nearly every battle, starting with the very first at Bunker Hill. Several African American **regiments** came from New England states.

Vocabulary

regiment, n. a unit in the army

Chapter 16
Raising America's Spirits

> **The Big Question**
>
> What is meant by the statement, "Washington's plan for winning the war required patience"?

An Early British Victory Things went badly for the Continental Army during the early part of the war. Hardly three months after Americans celebrated the *Declaration of Independence*, a large British army assembled in New York City to do battle with Washington's still untrained army.

The British defeated the Continental Army easily. It almost trapped them. That might have ended the war then and there. Led by Washington, however, some of the American forces escaped.

It was during that battle for New York City that a twenty-four-year-old Connecticut schoolteacher named Nathan Hale became famous. Hale was caught serving as a spy for the Americans and was hanged by the British. His last words were, "I only regret that I have but one life to lose for my country." His words **inspired** the Patriots. His words are still quoted today.

> **Vocabulary**
>
> **inspire,** v. to cause someone to think or behave in a certain way

Nathan Hale was executed by the British for spying for the Americans.

After the Continental Army's narrow escape from New York, the Americans retreated across New Jersey and into Pennsylvania. The British stayed close behind. Luckily, it was getting late in the year. Winter was a hard time to fight battles. The British were satisfied to take control of New York and New Jersey, and settle in for the winter. They could finish off the Americans in the spring. It was at this moment that Washington's leadership began to pay off. Other generals might have panicked after such a setback, but not Washington. Whether he won a battle or lost, he remained steady. Soldiers admired him and were willing to follow him into battle.

Battle, however, was not what Washington wanted. He knew his untrained troops were no match for the experienced British army head-on in a battle. Washington's plan for winning the war required patience. Instead of taking on the British directly, Washington's strategy was like Thomas Paine's checkerboard. He would keep the Continental Army moving. They would stop and fight the British now and then, but they would not get into a major battle. This way, Washington could buy time to build and train his army.

Washington's plan meant the Continental Army would not win many battles. They wouldn't lose many battles either. Meanwhile, as the war went on, the British people might tire of paying for it. After a few big American victories, who knew? Maybe the British would stop supporting the war altogether!

A Surprise Attack

Washington realized that the American people could tire of the war too. So could his army, if it kept suffering defeats. Washington needed a quick victory, or two, to raise the spirits of his soldiers and of the rest of the nation.

Washington planned a surprise attack on British mercenaries, the soldiers the British hired from other countries. The mercenaries were called Hessians, because many came from the **German state** of Hesse. The Hessians were camped in Trenton, New Jersey, just across the Delaware River from Pennsylvania.

> **Vocabulary**
>
> **"German state,"** (phrase), one of several small, independent states that eventually made up the present-day country of Germany

Washington planned to take the Hessians by surprise. After all, who would suspect the Continental Army to row across the ice-filled Delaware River in the dead of winter? On Christmas Night, 1776, shivering American soldiers stepped into the rowboats that would carry them across the river. By four o'clock in the morning, all 2,400 of Washington's men were on the New Jersey side of the river.

The Continental Army marched the nine miles to Trenton hidden by the darkness of night. As day broke, they attacked the sleeping Hessians. Caught off guard, the Hessians were surprised and confused. After a short fight, nine hundred Hessians surrendered.

This famous painting by Emmanuel Leutze of *Washington crossing the Delaware River* was painted many years after the event.

The Continental Army captured not only the enemy soldiers, but also their weapons and supplies.

Eight days later, Washington won another victory. Again, he used the element of surprise, this time to defeat British soldiers in

Princeton, New Jersey. Just as Washington hoped, the victories at Trenton and Princeton raised American spirits, especially for the men fighting in the Continental Army.

Chapter 17
Saratoga

Britain's Master Plan American spirits wouldn't stay high for very long. Not if the British could help it. In fact, British generals had a plan to knock the Americans out of the war before the year was over.

The Big Question

What mistake did the British make that brought France into the war, making an American victory possible?

The Hudson River Valley was an important part of Britain's plan for victory.

Vocabulary

rebels, n. people who resist the government with force

The Hudson River runs north and south in New York State. The British aimed to win control of the entire Hudson River Valley. If the British controlled the Hudson, they could cut off New England from the other states, dividing the Americans in two. The British would then be able to defeat the **rebels** one part at a time. They would defeat New England first and then the rest of the states.

That summer, General John Burgoyne (/bur*goyn/) led a large British army southward from Canada into New York State. The plan was for the main British army in New York City to start moving north soon after Burgoyne entered New York State. At about the same time, a third, smaller British force in western New York State would move east. The three British armies would meet near Albany, on the Hudson River. At that point, it would be all over for the upstart Americans.

That never happened. General William Howe was in charge of the main British army in New York. Howe wanted to capture Philadelphia first *before* moving north along the Hudson. Philadelphia was America's largest city. It was the meeting place of the Continental Congress. What a blow to American spirits if the British were to take it!

Howe was sure he could capture Philadelphia and still have time to meet Burgoyne. He was wrong. By the time he captured Philadelphia, there was no time left to get back to New York. Howe didn't even try.

Meanwhile, the third British force—the one moving eastward across New York State—ran into Continental Army soldiers along the way. This British force, which included a large number of Native American allies, never made it to Albany either.

That left Burgoyne and his army alone, moving south in New York State. The only ones there to meet him were General Gates and thousands of soldiers of the Continental Army. In October 1777, the British and Americans fought at Saratoga, north of Albany. The Americans won. Six thousand of Great Britain's best soldiers surrendered.

It was a great moment when General Gates accepted General Burgoyne's surrender after the Battle of Saratoga.

New Allies

The victory at Saratoga was a great turning point of the war. Not just because it was a great victory but also because it brought the Americans a new ally—France. Remember how the French and the English had been fighting for a hundred years? Remember how the French lost all their North American colonies to Great Britain in the French and Indian War? Well, ever since, they had been burning for revenge.

One way for France to get revenge on Great Britain was to help the American colonies break away. Soon after the colonies declared their independence, France secretly started sending them money and supplies.

The money and supplies helped, but the Americans hoped for more. They wanted France to jump into the war with both feet. Every time they asked the French to join in the fight, however, they got the same answer. France would not enter the war unless the Americans proved that they had a real chance of defeating the British.

Vocabulary

"naval fleet," (phrase), a large group of war ships that belong to the navy

The victory at Saratoga showed France that America could win. Several months after the Battle of Saratoga, the French entered the war on the side of the Americans. France sent money, equipment, and soldiers. Most importantly, France also sent a large **naval fleet** to help the Americans. It's quite possible that without help from the French, the Americans would not have won the war.

Eventually, Spain and the Netherlands also declared war against the British. This **turn of events** happened because three British armies failed to meet as planned in Albany.

Vocabulary

"turn of events," (phrase), a new development or action that changes the way future events happen

Chapter 18
Valley Forge

A Hard Winter The winter of 1777–1778 was the worst time of the war for the Continental Army. The British had taken Philadelphia.

The Big Question

What were some of the challenges the Continental Army faced during the winter at Valley Forge?

Twice, General Washington had sent his soldiers into battle near Philadelphia. Twice the British had defeated them. With cold weather coming on, Washington had to choose a place to camp for the winter. The place he chose was called Valley Forge, an open field about twenty-five miles northeast of Philadelphia.

Snow was already on the ground when the soldiers arrived in Valley Forge. They put up their tents and began building huts with whatever wood they could find. Before long, they had built two thousand of them. The huts were drafty, dirty, and cold but they at least put a roof over the soldiers' heads. Each hut had a fireplace but no windows. The smoke from the fires made men cough as if their lungs would burst.

Vocabulary

scarce, adj. in short supply; not having enough

The winter in Valley Forge was terrible. Supplies did not arrive. Blankets were **scarce**. There was not enough food. With no boots or shoes, the men wrapped their feet in rags.

The winter at Valley Forge could have broken the spirit of the Continental Army.

General Washington later said, "You might have tracked the army to Valley Forge by the blood of their feet." An officer from Connecticut explained how bad conditions were in his journal:

> It snows. I'm sick. Eat nothing. . . . No **forage**. Lord, Lord, Lord . . . cold and uncomfortable. I am sick, discontented, and out of humor. Poor food. Hard lodging. Cold weather. Fatigue. Nasty clothes. Nasty cookery. . . . Smoked out of my senses. . . . I can't endure it. Why are we sent here to starve and freeze?

Vocabulary

forage, n. food or other items found in a search

exposure, n. harm caused by cold or other extreme weather conditions

character, n. the qualities that make up a person

At least 2,500 soldiers died of disease or from **exposure** at Valley Forge that winter. That means that every single day, soldiers had to bury twenty-five or thirty of their comrades. Some men deserted, which means they simply sneaked out of camp and went home. At the start of winter, Washington's army numbered about seven thousand men. By the end of winter, there were only about four thousand left.

A Man of Character

What did people mean when they said that George Washington was a man of great **character**? They meant he was honest. They meant that he cared for his men, and that he was fair with them. They meant that people always knew where Washington stood and that he kept his word. They meant that he respected others. They meant that Washington was someone you would want on your side.

Washington also knew enough to put able men in charge of important tasks. For example, in February, when things were at their worst, a balding, red-faced man appeared at Washington's headquarters to offer his services. His name was Baron Frederick von Steuben (/stoo*bun/). Washington could tell that von Steuben knew how to train men to be soldiers. That was exactly what Washington needed. He hired von Steuben. The German officer taught the men about soldiering. He **drilled** them over and over. By spring, General Washington had a well-trained army for the very first time.

Von Steuben was only one of a number of Europeans inspired to help the American cause. Another was a nineteen-year-old Frenchman named the Marquis (/mar*key/) de Lafayette. As soon as he heard that fighting had begun in America, Lafayette joined the Americans. "I am persuaded," he said, "that the human race was created to be free, and that I am born to serve that cause." Washington took a liking to this daring Frenchman. Lafayette quickly became one of his most trusted **aides**.

Vocabulary

drill, v. to train or practice by repeating movements or tasks

aide, n. a trusted assistant

Baron von Steuben helped train American troops.

Chapter 19
Fighting Shifts to the South

> **The Big Question**
>
> Why did the British shift the fighting to the South?

Another Plan While the Continental Army regrouped at Valley Forge, the British generals made another plan to win the war. For three years, the British had been fighting the Americans in the North. They had won nearly all of the battles, so they weren't losing the war. But that didn't mean they were winning it either.

To win, the British would have to beat down the rebellion. They would have to really defeat the Continental Army. Every time the British had a chance to do that, though, General Washington and his army managed to slip away.

British military leaders were frustrated in their efforts to defeat the Continental Army.

The British generals thought: Suppose we shift the battle to the South? That would give us several advantages. For one thing, most of the Continental Army is in the North. We will catch them off guard. Also, there are many Loyalists in the South, including enslaved African Americans. They will help us with food and supplies. After we take the South, we'll have the Continental Army squeezed between our forces there and our forces in the North.

The plan was pretty successful for a while. The British navy brought soldiers from their base in New York to Savannah, Georgia. The soldiers quickly captured the city. Within a year, they controlled the whole state of Georgia. Soon after, the British took Charleston, South Carolina, and handed the Americans their worst defeat of the war. From there, British troops successfully went on to control a large part of the South.

However, the British were still not able to crush their enemy. American military commanders in the South followed George Washington's strategy. Small battles, yes. Big battles, no. Never risk the whole army in one big fight. Also, Southerners knew their land better than the British did. They set up secret bases in the **swamps** of South Carolina. They came out of the swamps to attack small groups of British soldiers. Then, as suddenly as they had appeared, they were gone. Even though there were no large-scale battles, the fighting was at times fierce, with many casualties and some acts of cruelty.

Vocabulary

swamp, n. a wet, marshy area where water collects

This kind of hit-and-run fighting is called **guerrilla warfare**. A general named Francis Marion was so successful at it that he became known as the Swamp Fox. The British armies won many small battles, but they could never catch up to the American forces to defeat them in a big one. In time, the Americans began to win their share of the battles.

> **Vocabulary**
>
> **"guerrilla warfare,"** (phrase), fighting in small groups making small, repeated attacks
>
> **tributary,** n. a stream or river that flows into a larger stream, a river, or a lake
>
> **company,** n. a unit in the military made up of anywhere from 80 to 250 soldiers

War in the West

Meanwhile, in the West, a young Virginian named George Rogers Clark attacked several British forts that had been built near **tributaries** of the Ohio River. The British had used their presence and their interest in trade in the West to gain support from Native Americans. However, American settlers saw the British and the Native Americans as a threat.

On July 4, 1778, Clark and a **company** of 175 Virginia militiamen captured the first of the British forts without firing a single shot. Later, Clark captured two more. His victories drove the British out of part of the land between the Appalachian Mountains and the Mississippi River.

A Victory at Sea

The tiny American navy, of course, was no match for the great British fleet. Still, American warships put up a good fight when they met one British ship at a time. John Paul Jones was the commander of the American ship *Bonhomme* (/bahn*um/) *Richard* when it came upon the British warship *Serapis* off the coast of Great Britain. The two ships opened fire. Soon the deck of the American ship was in flames. The British commander then demanded that Jones surrender. Jones replied, "I have not yet begun to fight!"

And fight he did. His own ship, the *Bonhomme Richard*, sank, but not before Jones and his men climbed aboard the *Serapis* and took it over. This became one of the most famous **naval battles** in United States history.

Vocabulary

"naval battle," (phrase), a military battle fought on water using warships

The sea battle between the *Bonhomme Richard* and the *Serapis* took over four hours.

Benedict Arnold

During this time, George Washington suffered one of his greatest disappointments. It was not a defeat on the battlefield. It was a defeat of the spirit. One of the Patriots' bravest and finest generals, and one of Washington's favorites, went over to the enemy.

His name was Benedict Arnold. Arnold had helped win the Battle of Saratoga. He had been promoted to general. His future in the American army was bright. In 1780, General Washington placed Benedict Arnold in command of West Point, a fort on the Hudson River.

Despite his success, Benedict Arnold did not feel appreciated enough. He also liked to spend more money than he could afford on luxuries. So in exchange for a large sum of money, Arnold agreed to turn over West Point to the British.

The plot was discovered in time, but Arnold himself escaped and joined the British forces. Americans were shocked to learn of Benedict Arnold's **treason**.

Vocabulary

treason, n. disloyalty to a country by helping an enemy

Chapter 20
The World Turned Upside Down

A British Mistake Then Great Britain made a mistake that cost it the war. The general in charge of the British armies in the South was Lord Charles Cornwallis. Cornwallis spent a year chasing the Continental Army in the South.

The Big Question

How does the chapter title explain the outcome of the American Revolution?

Then came the battle of Kings Mountain, along the North and South Carolina border. At Kings Mountain, the Continental Army defeated a large Loyalist force. Cornwallis realized the British plan for the South would not work. He decided to move his army to Virginia. If he could defeat the Continental Army in Virginia, he would crush the rebellion.

In the summer of 1781, Cornwallis chose a small Virginia town called Yorktown for his base. Yorktown is located on the York River, which flows into the sea. At Yorktown, the British navy could bring Cornwallis troops and supplies.

D' YORK

Bâtiments Anglois

Bâtiments Anglois coulés à fonds pour boucher le Chenal

YORK

Seconde paralelle ouverte la nuit du 11 au 12

Première Paralelle ouverte la nuit du 6 au 7

More Houbse

Dépot de la Tranchée Françoise

Dépot de la Tranchée Américaine

Brigade du Gal. de la Fayette

Brigade du Gal. Lincoln

Gal. Clinton

Map of the Battle of Yorktown

Normally, it's not a good idea to set up a base with a river behind you. If you have to retreat, you have no place to go. But Cornwallis felt safe there. He had one third of all the British soldiers in America with him. The British navy would bring him even more, if he needed them.

Washington Responds

While Cornwallis set up his base at Yorktown, George Washington was meeting with a French general in Rhode Island. The French general, Rochambeau (/row*sham*bow/), had brought an army to help the Americans. A large French fleet was on its way.

Washington and Rochambeau planned to attack the British armies in New York City. Then the news about Yorktown arrived.

Washington immediately saw Cornwallis's mistake. Forget about attacking New York, he said. The American and French armies should hurry to Virginia. Together, they had enough men to trap Cornwallis. If the French fleet could get there in time, it could keep the British navy from helping Cornwallis. Then Cornwallis would have to surrender. In one single victory, Washington might end the war! Yorktown was five hundred miles away. George Washington started his military career with a four-hundred-mile journey. That first journey ended in disappointment. This second opportunity could be the victory of a lifetime.

It took more than a month for the American and French armies to reach Yorktown. It took a few more days to dig a great half ring of trenches around the town. On October 9, at five o'clock in the afternoon, the first cannon was fired. The Battle of Yorktown had begun. For once, General Washington had the most guns and cannons. For once, General Washington had the most men.

Cornwallis looked to the sea for help. None came. The French fleet had driven off the British fleet. Cornwallis's army was on its own.

Each day, Washington moved his army closer, tightening the half ring around Yorktown. Washington rode among his men, despite the risk that a bullet might strike him. His soldiers cheered and pressed on.

Cornwallis was trapped. For several more days, American cannons roared. Finally, the British general saw that it was useless to continue. On October 17, 1781, Cornwallis surrendered.

The American Revolution ended soon after the surrender at Yorktown.

Two days later the American and French armies formed two long lines. The defeated British forces marched between them and left the town. As they did, a British army band played the tune of a nursery rhyme. A strange tune to play at a time like this, but the words made sense to the British:

If buttercups buzzed after the bee,

If boats were on land, churches on sea,

If ponies rode men, and if grass ate the corn

And cats should be chased into holes by the mouse,

If the mammas sold babies for ***half a crown****,*

If summer were spring, and the other way 'round,

Then all the world would be upside down.

A group of citizen-soldiers had defeated one of the world's greatest armies. A group of colonies had won independence from a mother country for the first time in history. The United States of America had been created. The great British Empire had been humbled. In the peace treaty that followed, Britain agreed that the colonies were now "free and independent states."

Vocabulary

half a crown, n. a unit of money used by the British during the time of the American Revolution

A Final Word

The American Revolution produced many heroes such as John Paul Jones and Francis Marion. George Washington, the famous general, became known as the "Father of Our Country" for his leadership during the war and after. Most of the heroes, though, were ordinary people. Their names are not written in the history books. They were the Minutemen on Lexington Green. They were the soldiers who shivered at Valley Forge. They were the men who dashed out of their swamp hideouts to strike at the British army.

They were also the women who brought food and water to the men in battle. They were the women who took care of the wounded and the sick. They were the women who kept farms and shops running. They were the farm families who shared their food with American soldiers and the townspeople who gave them housing. They were the women, children, and old men who made weapons and gunpowder for the Continental Army. They were the children who helped produce the food and clothing that the American soldiers needed to survive.

When the war was over, people everywhere asked, "How could the American colonies have won a war against one of the greatest military powers in the world?" The answer was not difficult to find. The Revolutionary War was won because ordinary Americans refused to lose it.

The Thirteen English Colonies of North America

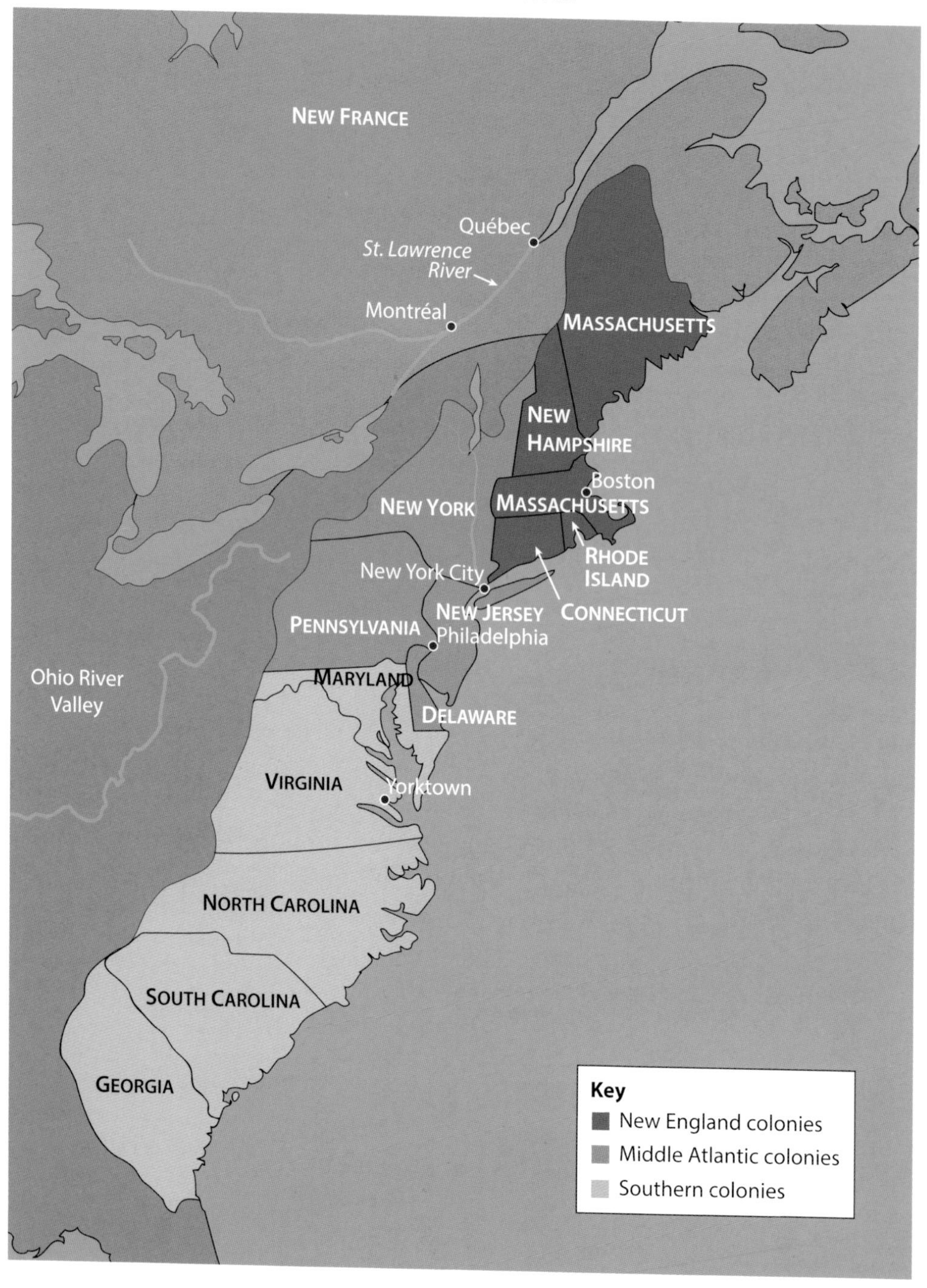

Colonial North America After the French and Indian War

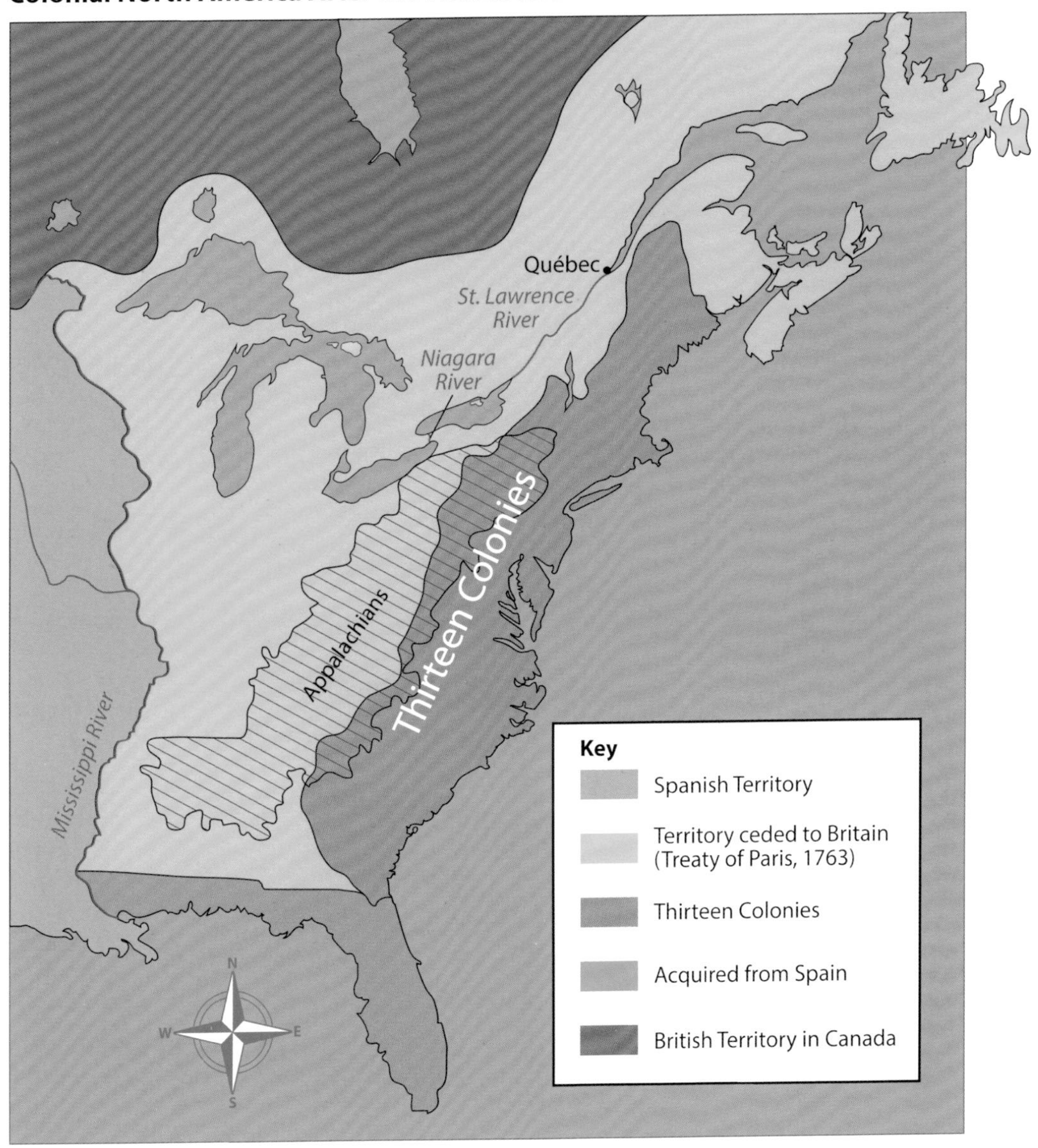

Revolutionary War Battles

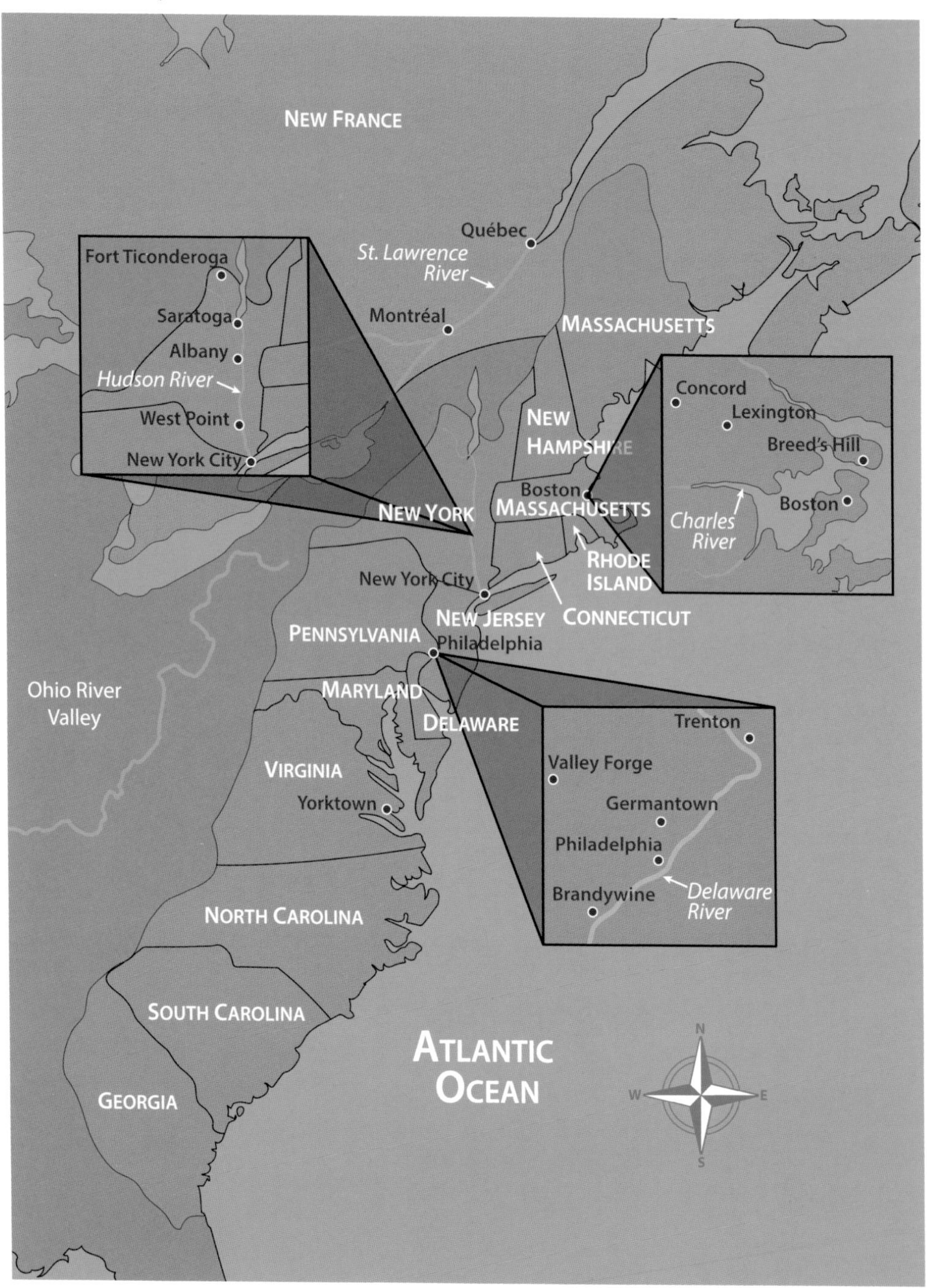

Glossary

A

advance, v. to move forward (34)

aide, n. a trusted assistant (115)

ally, n. a nation that promises to help another nation in wartime (30)

ammunition, n. bullets or shells (86)

assembly, n. a group of representatives who gather to make laws (21)

B

boycott, n. a form of organized protest in which people refuse to buy goods or have anything to do with a particular group or country (47)

brethren, n. members of the same group or family (76)

C

character, n. the qualities that make up a person (114)

citizen, n. a person who is legally recognized as a member or subject of a country or state (23)

colonel, n. a high-ranking military official (34)

colony, n. an area, region, or country that is controlled and settled by people from another country (2)

committee, n. a group of people selected to do a certain task (60)

company, n. a unit in the military made up of anywhere from 80 to 250 soldiers (119)

Congress, n. the law-making branch of the American government that is made up of the House of Representatives and the Senate (20)

"course of action," (phrase), a plan to respond to a situation (48)

custom, n. a traditional way of acting or doing something (6)

D

declaration, n. a formal statement (70)

defiant, adj. breaking the rules on purpose (71)

disease, n. sickness (15)

drill, v. to train or practice by repeating movements or tasks (115)

E

empire, n. a group of countries or territories, ruled by an all-powerful authority such as a monarch (18)

endow, v. to give someone something valuable (92)

English Parliament, n. the original law-making branch of the English government that is made up of the House of Lords and the House of Commons (20)

engraving, n. a design or pattern that is cut into the surface of an object (55)

enslaved, adj. forced to become a slave (13)

exposure, n. harm caused by cold or other extreme weather conditions (114)

F

forage, n. food or other items found in a search (114)

fort, n. a protected building or place that is generally used by the military as a stronghold (26)

frontier, n. where newly settled areas adjoin unsettled areas or the wilderness (6)

G

general, n. the main leader of an army (29)

"German state," (phrase), one of several small, independent states that eventually made up the present-day country of Germany (103)

governor, n. a person appointed by the king to oversee a region or colony (26)

"guerrilla warfare," (phrase), fighting in small groups making small, repeated attacks (119)

H

half a crown, n. a unit of money used by the British during the time of the American Revolution (126)

harbor, n. a part of a body of water that is next to land and provides a safe place for ships to anchor (52)

herb, n. a plant used to give food flavor or as medicine (15)

I

immigrant, n. a person from one country who moves to another country to live (2)

import, v. to bring in goods to one country from another country (42)

independence, n. freedom from the control of a person or group of people (24)

inspire, v. to cause someone to think or behave in a certain way (100)

institute, v. to establish or start something (93)

intolerable, adj. unbearable (66)

K

"kill two birds with one stone," (idiom), to accomplish two different things at the same time (77)

L

Loyalist, n. a person living in the colonies who did not support the American cause and remained loyal to Great Britain (88)

M

manufacturer, n. a person or company that makes or produces an item to be sold (52)

massacre, n. the violent killing of defenseless people (55)

mercenary, n. a soldier from one country paid to fight for another country (94)

merchant, n. a person who sells or trades goods (5)

migrate, v. to move from one place to another to live (4)

militia, n. a group of armed citizens prepared for military service at any time (26)

Minutemen, n. people who volunteered to serve in the American militia and were ready to fight at a moment's notice (77)

molasses, n. thick, dark, sticky syrup made from sugar (42)

N

"naval battle," (phrase), a military battle fought on water using warships (120)

"naval fleet," (phrase), a large group of war ships that belong to the navy (110)

O

oppose, v. to be against something (66)

P

pamphlet, n. a small booklet that includes information or ideas about a single topic (90)

parade, n. a public display of people moving in a long line (34)

Patriot, n. a person who supported the cause of the colonists during the American Revolution (48)

"peace treaty," (phrase), an agreement between two or more groups to bring an end to fighting, conflict, or war between themselves (36)

petition, n. a formal written request for change signed by several people (82)

plantation, n. a large farm where cash crops are grown by the person who owns the land (13)

policy, n. an official course of action (82)

prime minister, n. the head of the government in some countries (35)

proclamation, n. an important official announcement that is usually made to the public (40)

Q

quill pen, n. a pen made from the feather of a bird (60)

R

rebels, n. people who resist the government with force (108)

redcoat, n. a nickname given to British soldiers because of the color of their uniforms (78)

regiment, n. a unit in the army (99)

repeal, v. to cancel or do away with something, such as a law (49)

representative, n. a person who is chosen or elected to speak on the behalf of other people (21)

resist, v. to go against (67)

resistance, n. an effort to stop a law or policy from taking effect (49)

resolution, n. a final decision usually meant to solve a problem or create a course of action (71)

revolution, n. the act of overthrowing a government with the hopes of starting a new and different one (93)

S

scarce, adj. in short supply; not having enough (112)

self-government, n. the ability of people to rule themselves and make their own laws (20)

silversmith, n. a person who makes things out of silver (55)

stockpile, n. a large amount of something being stored for future use (80)

Supreme Court, n. the highest court in the land (70)

swamp, n. a wet, marshy area where water collects (118)

T

tax, n. money that people are required to pay to support the workings of the government (20)

tax collector, n. a person appointed by the government who is responsible for collecting taxes from citizens (42)

"taxation without representation," (phrase), the idea that American colonists did not have a say in the English Parliament, which enacted taxes without their consent (46)

trade, n. the exchange or sale of goods or services. (5)

treason, n. disloyalty to a country by helping an enemy (121)

trench, n. a narrow ditch dug into the ground (86)

tributary, n. a stream or river that flows into a larger stream, a river, or a lake (119)

"turn of events," (phrase), a new development or action that changes the way future events happen (111)

U

unfurl, v. to unroll and spread out like a piece of fabric or a flag (80)

V

"village green," (phrase), an open grassy area in a village or town (79)

CKHG™

Core Knowledge History and Geography™

Series Editor-In-Chief

E.D. Hirsch, Jr.

Editorial Directors

Linda Bevilacqua and Rosie McCormick

Subject Matter Expert

J. Chris Arndt, PhD, Department of History, James Madison University

Illustration and Photo Credits

ACME Imagery / ACME Imagery / Superstock: 59

A General View of the City of London next to the River Thames, c.1780 (engraving), English School, 18th c/ Private Collection / Bridgeman Images: 56–57

Bryan Beus: 3

Bunker's Hill, 1775, c.1900 (w/c on paper) by Richard Simkin (1840–1926) / National Army Museum, London / Bridgeman Images: 87

Daniel Hughes: 21, 63, 82–83

David Sheldon: 48

Declaration of Independence, 1776, 1st January 1823 (facsimile on vellum) by William James Stone (1798–1865) / Gilder Lehrman Collection, New York, USA / Bridgeman Images: 91

Durga Benhard: 14, 50–51

Everett Collection / Everett / Superstock: 89B

General George Washington (1732–99) at Yorktown, Virginia by James Peale (1749–1831) / Private Collection / Peter Newark American Pictures / Bridgeman Images: Cover B, 84

George Washington in the uniform of a Colonel of the Virginia Militia during the French & Indian War (1755–63) by Charles Willson Peale (1741–1827) / Private Collection / Peter Newark American Pictures / Bridgeman Images: 29

Gideon Kendall: 11, 25, 69

Jacob Wyatt: 33

Jed Henry: 72, 79

Last Words of Captain Nathan Hale , pub. 1858 (hand coloured engraving) by Alexander Hay Ritchie (1822–1895) / Private Collection / The Stapleton Collection / Bridgeman Images: 101

Map of the Siege of York in 1781, from 'Guerre de l'Amerique', 1782 (colour engraving) by F. Dubourg (fl.1780–82) / Service Historique de la Marine, Vincennes, France / Bridgeman Images: 122–123

Michelle Weaver: 12

Patrick Henry speaking to Virginia delegates in 1775 by Louis S.Glanzman (b.1922) / National Geographic Creative / Bridgeman Images: 75

Red Coat Soldiers Toasting The Ladies Of The House by Howard Pyle/WikiArt: 43

Retribution: Tarring and Feathering, or The Patriot's Revenge, published by Hannah Humphrey in 1795 (hand–coloured etching) by James Gillray (1757–1815) / © Courtesy of the Warden and Scholars of New College, Oxford / Bridgeman Images: 67

Scott Hammond: Cover A, Cover C, Cover D, i, ii, 1, 26–27, 35, 41, 44–45, 47, 54, 65, 71, 71, 85, 95, 97, 98

Sharae Peterson: 38–39

Shari Griffiths: 7

SuperStock / SuperStock: 106–107, 109, 112–113, 115

Surrender of Cornwallis at Yorktown, 19 October 1781 by John Trumbull (1756–1843) / Private Collection / Peter Newark American Pictures / Bridgeman Images: 125

Take Notice', American Revolutionary War recruitment poster, American School,18th c/ Private Collection / Peter Newark Military Pictures / Bridgeman Images: 96

The House of Commons in Session, 1710 (oil on canvas) by Peter Tillemans (1684–1734) / Houses of Parliament, Westminster, London, UK / Bridgeman Images: 19

Thomas Paine (oil on canvas) by Bass Otis (1784–1861) / Huntington Library and Art Gallery, San Marino, CA, USA / ©The Huntington Library, Art Collections & Botanical Gardens / Bridgeman Images: 89A

Tyler Pack: 5

Universal Images Group / Superstock: 117, 120

Washington Crossing the Delaware River, 25th December 1776, 1851 (oil on canvas) (copy of an original painted in 1848) by Emanuel Gottlieb Leutze (1816–68) / Metropolitan Museum of Art, New York, USA / Bridgeman Images: 104–105